SOCCER SUPERSTARS

2000-2001

SOCCER SUPERSTARS

2000-2001

p

This is a Parragon Book
First published in 2000

Parragon
Queen Street House
4 Queen Street
Bath BA1 1HE, UK

ISBN 0 75254 079 3

Conceived, designed and produced by
Hazar Publishing, London

Acknowledgements
Words: Tim Hill
Designer: John Dunne

CONTENTS

INTRODUCTION			8
DAVID BECKHAM	MANCHESTER UNITED	ENGLAND	10
DENNIS BERGKAMP	ARSENAL	HOLLAND	12
MICHAEL BRIDGES	LEEDS UNITED		14
TITI CAMARA	LIVERPOOL	GUINEA	16
KEVIN CAMPBELL	EVERTON		18
ANDY COLE	MANCHESTER UNITED	ENGLAND	20
JOE COLE	WEST HAM UNITED		22
TONY COTTEE	LEICESTER CITY	ENGLAND	24
BRIAN DEANE	MIDDLESBROUGH	ENGLAND	26
PAOLO DI CANIO	WEST HAM UNITED	ITALY	28
DION DUBLIN	ASTON VILLA	ENGLAND	30
DUNCAN FERGUSON	NEWCASTLE UNITED	SCOTLAND	32
TORE ANDRE FLO	CHELSEA	NORWAY	34
ROBBIE FOWLER	LIVERPOOL	ENGLAND	36
RYAN GIGGS	MANCHESTER UNITED	WALES	38
DAVID GINOLA	TOTTENHAM HOTSPUR	FRANCE	40
SHAUN GOATER	MANCHESTER CITY	BERMUDA	42
THIERRY HENRY	ARSENAL	FRANCE	44
EMILE HESKEY	LIVERPOOL	ENGLAND	46
ANDY HUNT	CHARLTON ATHLETIC		48
STEFFEN IVERSEN	TOTTENHAM HOTSPUR	NORWAY	50

Name	Club	Country	Page
FRANCIS JEFFERS	EVERTON	ENGLAND	52
JULIAN JOACHIM	ASTON VILLA	ENGLAND	54
NWANKWO KANU	ARSENAL	NIGERIA	56
ROBBIE KEANE	COVENTRY CITY	EIRE	58
HARRY KEWELL	LEEDS UNITED	AUSTRALIA	60
GEORGIOU KINKLADZE	DERBY COUNTY	GEORGIA	62
PAUL MERSON	ASTON VILLA	ENGLAND	64
MARC OVERMARS	ARSENAL	HOLLAND	66
MICHAEL OWEN	LIVERPOOL	ENGLAND	68
MARIAN PAHARS	SOUTHAMPTON	LATVIA	70
EMMANUEL PETIT	ARSENAL	FRANCE	72
KEVIN PHILLIPS	SUNDERLAND	ENGLAND	74
GUSTAVO POYET	CHELSEA	URUGUAY	76
NIALL QUINN	SUNDERLAND	EIRE	78
SERGEI REBROV	TOTTENHAM HOTSPUR	UKRAINE	80
HAMILTON RICARD	MIDDLESBROUGH	COLOMBIA	82
ALAN SHEARER	NEWCASTLE UNITED	ENGLAND	84
OLE GUNNAR SOLSKJAER	MANCHESTER UNITED	NORWAY	88
PAULO WANCHOPE	WEST HAM UNITED	COSTA RICA	90
DWIGHT YORKE	MANCHESTER UNITED	TRINIDAD&TOBAGO	92
GIANFRANCO ZOLA	CHELSEA	ITALY	94

British football has always been unbeatable for high-octane excitement

The criticism used to be that it was excitement
at the expense of quality. Not any more. With the likes of Owen, Zola,
Bergkamp, Di Canio and Kewell, English football oozes the kind of
class to rival that of any league in the world. Football
here today is for the passionate and the purist.

Nor has any other league such strength across all divisions.
Chelsea's superstars can beat mighty Barcelona, but get
turned over by struggling Watford. Blackburn can take the league
title by storm, then find themselves languishing back in Division
One just a couple of years later. In British football the minnows can
scale the heights, while the giants can go into free fall.
Such unpredictability is what supporters' dreams are made of.

Within these pages are the players who will
make tomorrow's dreams come true. They are the top strikers and
attacking midfielders, the players who will be in the thick of the
goalmouth action in the coming season. The profiles will tell you
everything you need to know about these soccer superstars;
everything except which of them will score the vital goals that will
bring league and cup glory in 2000-2001.

All Premiership players live their lives in a goldfish bowl, but in recent years no one has found himself under the spotlight more than David Beckham. Not only does he play for the club with the highest profile, but with a celebrity wife and the memory of that infamous sending-off in France '98, Beckham has been subjected to the most intense scrutiny by the media and the most terrible abuse from rival fans.

Rising to the challenge

Some players' performances might have suffered under such pressure, but Beckham has risen to every challenge and let his feet do the talking. Who can forget the vision and precision he showed to beat Wimbledon's Neil Sullivan from the halfway line in the opening game of the 1996-97 season? Or, more recently, in this year's Champions' League quarter-final at Old Trafford, the way he danced through Real Madrid's defence and thundered the ball into the top corner of the net.

Dead-ball specialist

When he isn't lashing in one of his trademark spectacular strikes, Beckham is the playmaker supreme. He is acknowledged as probably the best crosser of a ball in world football. The wicked, curling balls that he whips into the box at pace are a defender's nightmare, but the kind of service that the likes of Yorke and Cole thrive on. His dead-ball kicks are legendary, making corners and free kicks a formidable weapon for both United and England. And from midfield he sprays passes all over the park, playing his team-mates in with inch-perfect passes that can turn defences around or split them wide open.

Beckham on top form

Beckham's temperament has been questioned, and he has certainly been guilty in the past of some rash moments. But he is showing much greater maturity and control these days. A good example of this was the game that was billed as the grudge return clash between Beckham and Diego Simeone. Simeone was the player involved when Beckham was red-carded against Argentina during their second-round match at France '98. The two came head-to-head in the Champions' League less than a year later, when Manchester United came up against Inter Milan. Beckham was on top form that day, United ran out 2-0 winners on their way to a marvellous treble, and the only thing Beckham and Simeone swapped was their shirts at the end of the game.

Beckham made a name for himself at an early age, winning a Bobby Charlton Soccer Skills award at the age of 12. He had trials at his local club, Leyton Orient, then attended Tottenham Hotspur's school of excellence before joining United as a trainee in 1991. He made his debut in September 1992, but it was not until the 1995-96 season that he became a first choice in United's midfield. He was handed his first senior international cap by Glenn Hoddle in September 1996, in a game against Moldova.

PLAYER PROFILE

FULL NAME	David Robert Joseph Beckham
DATE OF BIRTH	2 May 1975
BIRTHPLACE	Leytonstone, England
HEIGHT	6'0"
WEIGHT	11st 12lbs
POSITION	Midfielder
TRANSFERS	Signed as a trainee

	Appearances	Goals
League '99/2000	31	6
England	28	1

AWARDS Carling Premiership Player Of The Month (August 1996); Sky Sports/Panasonic Young Player 1996; Sky Sports/Panasonic Fans' Footballer 1996; PFA Young Player of the Year 1997; Sir Matt Busby Player of the Year 1997

CLUB HONOURS FA Youth Cup 1992; Premier League 1996, 1997, 1999, 2000; FA Cup 1996, 1999; Charity Shield 1996, 1997; European Cup 1999

INTERNATIONAL HONOURS England Youth, England Under 21; England

THE HEART OF ENGLAND'S MIDFIELD Now 25, Beckham has already achieved everything in club football. Even those rival fans who have baited him must be hoping that he will go on to be at the heart of England's assaults on the European Championships and World Cups in the years to come.

Arsene Wenger has remarked that his Arsenal side, star-studded though it is, lacks a certain quality when Dennis Bergkamp is missing. But although Wenger has built a formidable squad in his time at Highbury, the jewel in his team was brought to the club by Bruce Rioch. Bergkamp became the Gunners' record buy when Rioch signed him from Inter Milan in July 1995 for £7.5m. Rioch had a difficult time in the Arsenal hot seat, however, and lasted only ten months in the job.

Supremely gifted

His fate was not helped by the fact that Bergkamp took some time to settle. He failed to find the net in his first seven games, and some were already beginning to question the decision to bring him to the club. Bergkamp had had an unhappy spell at Inter, and it seemed that Arsenal fans were witnessing the hang-over from that period, when what they wanted to see was the supremely gifted player who had honed his skills at the famous Ajax academy.

Gunner Dennis

The doubters should have remembered that cream always rises to the top, and once Bergkamp broke his duck with two goals against Southampton in late September, he was on the road to becoming one of the all-time great players to pull on an Arsenal shirt.

Cool precision

His trademark instant control and cool precision (which earned him the nickname 'The Iceman') were never better exemplified than in his superb strike against Argentina in the World Cup quarter-final at France '98. It was voted BBC TV's Goal of the Tournament - some consolation for the player as Holland went out on penalties against Brazil in the semis.

Player of the year

The 1997-98 season was also memorable for Bergkamp as he was voted Player of the Year by both the PFA and the Football Writers - the first person to win both awards in the same year since John Barnes a decade earlier. His performances that season were hugely instrumental in helping Arsenal to a famous League and FA Cup double, although he was unlucky to miss out on a Cup Final appearance through injury. The mercurial Dutchman also scooped the Goal of the Season award for a terrific strike against Leicester, and finished third in FIFA's World Footballer of the Year poll.

Bergkamp's future

Arsenal fans will be relieved to hear that Bergkamp, now 31, has pledged his future to the club. However, as far as the forthcoming Champions' League campaign is concerned, Wenger will be faced with the perennial problem of some tricky away ties without Bergkamp's services, because of the player's fear of flying.

PLAYER PROFILE

FULL NAME	Dennis Nicolaas Maria Bergkamp
DATE OF BIRTH	18 May 1969
BIRTHPLACE	Amsterdam, Holland
HEIGHT	6'0"
WEIGHT	12st 5lbs
POSITION	Forward
TRANSFER	July 1995 from Inter Milan
FEE	£7.5 million

	Appearances	Goals
League '99/2000	27	6
Holland	70	36

AWARDS Dutch Topscorer 1991, 1992, 1993; Dutch Player of the Year 1992, 1993; English Player of the Year 1998; English Football Writers Footballer of the Year 1998; Goal of the Season Award 1997/8; Arsenal FC Player of the Year 1998

CLUB HONOURS Premier League 1998; Charity Shield 1998, 2000

INTERNATIONAL HONOURS Holland

SUBLIME SKILLS
In recent years, concerns have been expressed over the number of overseas players in the Premiership, particularly players who are either second rate or past their best. Dennis Bergkamp is a shining exception to that charge, and continues to grace the Premiership with his sublime skills.

DENNIS BERGKAMP

When David O'Leary paid £5m for Michael Bridges, anyone living beyond Wearside might have been forgiven for asking the question: Michael who? 21-year-old Bridges was born on Tyne and Wear and joined Sunderland on the strength of a very respected recommendation - for it came from none other than the scout who had spotted Alan Shearer.

Runaway success

As Peter Reid's side ran away with promotion from Division 1 in 1998-99, Bridges became increasingly frustrated at his lack of first-team opportunities. Quinn and Phillips were the players in possession and Bridges spent a lot of time on the bench. It was no surprise, therefore, that he managed just eight goals that season.

Making an impact

Bridges has the combination of Jimmy Floyd Hasselbaink's departure from Elland Road and David O'Leary's astuteness to thank for his emergence in the past year. When the unsettled Dutch striker departed for Atletico Madrid, it left O'Leary with £12m in the coffers to strengthen his team. £5m for the exciting young Darren Huckerby from Coventry must have seemed a terrific buy to the Leeds faithful, while the same kind of money for Bridges was almost certainly considered excessive. Yet it is Bridges who has made the bigger impact at Elland Road, while Huckerby has found himself on the bench much of the time.

Hat-trick hero

It didn't take Bridges long to make an impact at his new club. In only his second game, against Southampton at The Dell, he started repaying some of the investment with a brilliant hat-trick. The fact that he had just four chances in the match showed he had the kind of quality needed at the highest level. His form has already brought him international recognition. He has played for England at Under-21 level and looks a certainty to play an important part in the senior squad in the years ahead.

Facing Europe's best

For the moment, Bridges is just content to be part of an exciting young Leeds side team that has become many fans' second favourite team. O'Leary's fearless young stars now face the next step on the learning curve: playing in the coming season's Champions' League against Europe's best.

Striker's instinct

Tottenham had been interested in signing Bridges when he was unsettled at Sunderland. But even though he'd supported Spurs as a boy, he instinctively felt that White Hart Lane wasn't the right place for him. When he met O'Leary and saw the Elland Road set-up, on the other hand, he made up his mind very quickly.

PLAYER PROFILE

FULL NAME	Michael Bridges
DATE OF BIRTH	5 August 1978
BIRTHPLACE	Whitley Bay, England
HEIGHT	6'1"
WEIGHT	10st 11lbs
POSITION	Forward
TRANSFER	July 1999 from Sunderland
FEE	£5 million

	Appearances	Goals
League '99/2000	34	19
England Under-21	2	

CLUB HONOURS Division One 1996, 1999

INTERNATIONAL HONOURS England Schoolboy; England Youth; England Under-21

THE FIVE-MILLION-POUND MAN
Considering the going rate for the top strikers, especially young ones, that £5m for Michael Bridges is now beginning to look like an absolute steal.

MICHAEL BRIDGES

In just a single season at Anfield Titi Camara has proved himself to something of a talisman for the team. Of the nine Premiership matches where he got on the scoresheet, Liverpool won eight and drew the other. More important to Liverpool fans is the great contribution he has made in such a short space of time. His pace, power and sheer unpredictability won them over very quickly.

Crucial goals

Although he featured in 33 League games altogether, Camara played the full 90 minutes on just nine occasions. His strike record, therefore, is a lot better than it first appears. His goals were often crucial, too, earning Liverpool a vital point or turning a draw into a win.

Camara on target

When he scored in three successive games - beginning with a strike which earned the Reds a point at Southampton in late October - it started a fantastic run of Championship-winning form. Camara followed it up with the only goal of the game against West Ham, and was on target again in the next match, at home to Bradford.

Key role

It was a run that would last 20 matches, with Liverpool winning 14 and drawing 5. One of those wins came in February at Highbury, where Camara again got the only goal of the game. He thus played a big part in Liverpool's push for the title last season. Only a poor run of form at the beginning and end of the campaign prevented Gerard Houllier's men from giving Manchester United a better run for their money.

Camara in France

Camara learned his football playing with oranges in his native Guinea. At the age of 15 he moved to France, where he was soon snapped up by St Etienne. He spent five years at the club, and although he scored just 16 goals, he did well enough for another French side, Lens, to come in for him. Once again, his goalscoring record was nothing special, but one of the best French sides of recent years, Marseille, added him to their squad.

Attacking options

Competition for places was intense at Marseille, and Camara's first-team opportunities were limited. The 26-year-old Camara jumped at the chance of a move to Anfield in the summer of 1999. For Houllier's part, the French connection meant that he knew all about Camara's strengths, and Liverpool were in need of attacking options other than Fowler and Owen.

Explosive debut

Camara signalled his arrival on the Premiership scene with an explosive debut against Sheffield Wednesday on the opening day of the season. He partnered Robbie Fowler that day up front and started paying off some of the £2.6m fee immediately by hitting the winner.

Crowd-pleaser

In full flight and with the ball at his feet, Titi Camara has shown himself to be a real crowd-pleaser. Whether he can please the Liverpool manager enough, and make it impossible for him to leave the Guinean out of the side is another matter.

PLAYER PROFILE

FULL NAME	Aboubacar Camara
DATE OF BIRTH	17 November 1972
BIRTHPLACE	Conafry, Guinea
HEIGHT	6'0"
WEIGHT	13st 4lbs
POSITION	Forward
TRANSFER	July 1999 from Marseille
FEE	£2.6 million

	Appearances	Goals
League '99/2000	33	9

CAMARA'S FUTURE Camara has spoken warmly of his affection for the club, and the rapport he has already built up with the Anfield crowd. But, ominously, he has expressed his unhappiness at being in and out of the side. His desire for regular first-team football - the very reason why he left Marseille - has begun to frustrate him at Liverpool. And the arrival of Emile Heskey has given Houllier even more striking options.

TITI CAMARA

Andy Cole left Arsenal in March 1992 because manager George Graham felt that Kevin Campbell was the better prospect. Since then, Cole has gone on to enjoy an almost unbroken run of success, while Campbell's career has been a mixture of highs and lows.

Campbell's double

Campbell went to Highbury as an 18-year-old trainee. In his seven years at the club he enjoyed more success than a lot of players manage in an entire career. He was part of the team that won the FA Cup and League Cup "double" in 1993; and he was in the starting line-up for the memorable Cup Winners' Cup final win over Parma the following year. Alan Smith got the winning goal that night in Copenhagen, but Campbell contributed vital goals on the way to European glory. His pace, power and sharpness also brought him England Under-21 honours. He left Highbury just as Dennis Bergkamp was arriving at the club. His £3m move to Nottingham Forest provided him with a fresh challenge. And a challenge it was, for it came at a time when the Midlands club were not the force they once were.

23 goals and promotion

In the 1997-98 season, his third at the club, Campbell helped to spearhead the side to the Division One Championship. In that season he had struck up the division's most potent partnership, with the temperamental Dutch striker Pierre Van Hooijdonk. The pair hit 49 goals between them in that promotion-winning season, with Campbell scoring 23. The duo never got the chance to pit themselves against Premiership defences, though. Van Hooijdonk had a much-publicised spat with the club, while Campbell was sold before a ball was kicked in the 1998-99 season.

Goodison call

His £2.5m move to the Turkish side Trabzonspor proved to be disastrous. Campbell was treated badly, and was soon desperate to leave. Early in 1999, with his 29th birthday approaching, Campbell would probably have jumped at any lifeline back into British football. As it turned out, he was offered a dream move to Everton, albeit in a loan deal. The Goodison club was struggling terribly and in serious danger of relegation. Walter Smith had few resources and there was a hint of desperation as he turned to Campbell to provide some much-needed firepower for the run-in.

Campbell's purple patch

What happened next must have been beyond the wildest imagination of both manager and player. A rejuvenated Campbell hit a purple patch as soon as he arrived at Goodison. His nine goals in eight games, including a hat-trick against West Ham, went a long way towards keeping Everton up. Even though he had joined the club for only the last couple of months of the season, he still finished as the club's top scorer. His goals made him an instant hero on the blue side of Liverpool. Duncan Ferguson had been a hard act to follow as far as the Everton fans were concerned, but Campbell's displays in the Number 9 shirt won them over instantly.

PLAYER PROFILE

FULL NAME	Kevin Joseph Campbell
DATE OF BIRTH	4 February 1970
BIRTHPLACE	Lambeth, England
HEIGHT	6'1"
WEIGHT	13st 8lbs
POSITION	Forward
TRANSFER	14 July 1999 from Trabzonspor
FEE	£3 million

	Appearances	Goals
League '99/2000	26	12
England B	1	

CLUB HONOURS FA Youth Cup 1988; League Cup 1993; FA Cup 1993; Cup Winners' Cup 1994; Division One 1998

INTERNATIONAL HONOURS England Under-21, England B International

THE NEW SEASON Campbell grabbed 12 goals from just 26 starts last term; not quite the inspired form he was in when he joined Everton, but a pretty good return, nevertheless. If he stays clear of injury in the coming season, the 30-year-old has the quality to put away the chances that the much-improved Everton side are creating.

KEVIN CAMPBELL

Few strikers divide opinion more than Andy Cole. His goals-per-game record at Manchester United - and at Newcastle United and Bristol City before - is up there with the best. Everybody acknowledges the deadly, almost telepathic partnership he has formed with Dwight Yorke; yet it is Yorke who tends to get the plaudits for his superb skills.

Cole and England

Cole's all-round game has undoubtedly improved considerably in his five years at United, but there are those who question his ability at the highest level. These have included some of the Old Trafford faithful, but the issue was brought into the open by former England coach Glenn Hoddle. Hoddle famously criticised Cole for needing too many chances in front of goal before putting one away. On the other side of the fence, it is not only Ferguson who sings Cole's praises. Many respected figures within the game have expressed their bewilderment as to what Cole has to do to gain more international recognition.

Bargain buy

Cole began his career at Arsenal, but found opportunities at Highbury limited, a situation that wasn't helped by the fact that George Graham rated Kevin Campbell a better prospect. Cole was sold to Bristol City in 1992 for just £500,000. 20 goals in 41 games was the kind of record that was bound to attract attention, and Newcastle came in for him in March 1993. The £1.75m fee represented good business for Bristol City, but Newcastle certainly got a bargain.

Phenomenal strike rate

Cole immediately started banging in the goals for the Tyneside club at a phenomenal rate, helping them to win promotion to the Premiership in his first season. Peter Beardsley was the wrong side of 30 and had been allowed to leave both Liverpool and Everton, but he was still a top performer. Cole and Beardsley

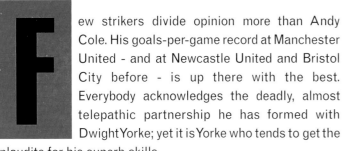

spearheaded an attractive, attacking side, and Cole has gone on record to say that, along with Yorke, Beardsley has been his favourite partner up front.

Cole and the Toon Army

The long-standing love affair that the Toon Army has with the club's prolific No 9s meant that Cole became an idol at St James' Park. No wonder, then, that there was anger and disbelief when Keegan agreed to sell him to - of all teams - Manchester United.

PLAYER PROFILE

FULL NAME	Andrew Alexander Cole
DATE OF BIRTH	15 October 1971
BIRTHPLACE	Nottingham, England
HEIGHT	5'11"
WEIGHT	11st 12lbs
POSITION	Forward
TRANSFER	12 January 1995 from Newcastle
FEE	£6 million

	Appearances	Goals
League '99/2000	28	19
England	7	

CLUB HONOURS
Division One 1993; Premier League 1996, 1997, 1999, 2000; FA Cup 1996, 1999; Charity Shield 1997; European Cup 1999

INTERNATIONAL HONOURS
England Schoolboy; England Youth; England Under-21; England B International; England

STRIKING FOR ENGLAND
Having achieved so much at club level with United, 28-year-old Cole's sights must surely be on England. Ironically, he was included in Hoddle's final England squad, but his chance of international honours must be greater with his old mentor Kevin Keegan in charge of the national team.

ANDY COLE

When Joe Cole limped out of West Ham's 2-1 win at Derby in April, following a crunching tackle by Rory Delap, it was initially thought to be just a case of severe bruising. A few days later, however, a scan revealed that it was a break, and any thoughts Cole had of making the Euro 2000 squad were dashed.

Precocious talent

Cole may not quite have made Kevin Keegan's final 22 for Holland and Belgium. On the other hand, the England coach is a known fan of Cole's precocious talent. And at 18, he is the same age that Michael Owen was when he burst on to the international scene two years ago.

Cole's quality

Cole and Owen played together in the same England Under-16 team. While Owen's meteoric rise has been well documented, Cole has progressed steadily through the ranks, to the England Under-18 and Under-21 sides. Few doubt that he will break through to senior level sooner or later. Keegan has spoken of his qualities: the way he sees things early; the ability he has to do the unexpected and make things happen. In short, Keegan sees Cole as a Gascoigne-type player who can turn matches single-handedly. Top international sides need such players, and most experts agree that England have been lacking that extra bit of quality since Gazza's decline. With such praise from the England coach himself, the senior squad must beckon for Cole in the not too distant future.

Young prodigy

Timing has been equally important as far as Cole's development at club level is concerned. West Ham boss Harry Redknapp also enthuses over his young prodigy,

but has tried to take the pressure off him by giving him a high squad number, and neither overpaying nor overplaying him. Last season he featured in 21 of West Ham's League matches before that fateful day at Pride Park, but played the full 90 minutes in only 14 games.

The Conjuror

Cole's view on how the game should be played fits exactly with West Ham's long and proud tradition for attacking, entertaining football. Indeed, the number of tricks he has up his sleeve has earned him the nickname "The Conjuror" among his team-mates. And his own footballing heroes are hardly surprising: Gascoigne himself and Eric Cantona. They were players who did things with the ball that other players couldn't, things that thrilled the crowds. There is no greater testimony to his talent than that of the many respected figures in the game who think he is out of the same mould as those two wonderful players.

PLAYER PROFILE

FULL NAME	Joseph John Cole
DATE OF BIRTH	8 November 1981
BIRTHPLACE	London, England
HEIGHT	5'9"
WEIGHT	11st 0lbs
POSITION	Midfielder
TRANSFER	Signed as a trainee

	Appearances	Goals
League '99/2000	22	1

CLUB HONOURS FA Youth Cup 1999

INTERNATIONAL HONOURS England Youth; England Under-21

HAMMER COLE

Cole was actually born quite close to Highbury, though he supported Chelsea as a youngster. The fact that he ended up at West Ham, rather than a rival London club - or any of the other top teams that were chasing him, for that matter - he puts down to the friendliness of the Upton Park set-up. He has been with the club since the age of 12 and is under contract there until 2004.

Tony Cottee is well known for the scrapbooks he keeps, detailing all the goals he has scored in his long career. In August 1997, when he was 32 and playing out in Malaysia for Selangor, Cottee must have thought that he wouldn't be needing many more of those scrapbooks. His career looked to be firmly on the downward path. Then Martin O'Neill stepped in to bring the veteran striker to Filbert Street for a bargain £500,000.

Returning to the big time

Although he was brought in mainly for cover and spent a lot of time on the bench during that 1997-98 season, he still made an excellent contribution. He got off the mark for the Foxes with a goal against Northampton in an FA Cup tie, then announced his return to the big time in the most emphatic way possible - by scoring the winner for Leicester against Manchester United at Old Trafford. With Ian Marshall injured, Cottee enjoyed a run in the side and rounded off the season by scoring twice against the club where he first made his name, West Ham.

Cottee's objectives

Cottee had been born in West Ham, and had two spells with the club, scoring 117 goals. Now, with this unexpected return to top-flight English football, Cottee set himself a new set of objectives: he wanted to reach the 200-goal mark, to play in a European competition, and to complete the set of scoring on every away ground in the Premiership.

Back in Europe

He realised one of those ambitions in that first season with Leicester as the club had qualified for the Cup Winners Cup. In his second season at Filbert Street Cottee hit 10 goals, his experience and poaching skills providing an excellent foil for the young, powerful Emile Heskey.

Dramatic winner

When Leicester went to Anfield in early May, Heskey was in the Liverpool side and Liverpool were desperate for points to secure a Champions' League spot. But it was Cottee who grabbed the headlines and Leicester who grabbed the points with a 2-1 win.

Cottee scored the opener after just two minutes, racing on to a Neil Lennon pass to slot the ball past Westerveld.

Fulfilled ambition

It was a double celebration for Cottee, for he not only set up the victory with his early strike, but he fulfilled that third ambition. For Anfield was the final ground on his hit-list, a ground he had never scored at in his 17 years as a professional. Cottee will be 35 going into the new season, but no doubt his next aim will be to beat last year's 13-goal haul. A new scrapbook needed, perhaps?

PLAYER PROFILE

FULL NAME	Anthony Richard Cottee
DATE OF BIRTH	11 July 1965
BIRTHPLACE	West Ham, England
HEIGHT	5'9"
WEIGHT	12st 6lbs
POSITION	Forward
TRANSFER	14 August 1997 from Selangor, Malaysia
FEE	£500,000

	Appearances	Goals
League '99/2000	33	13
England	7	

CLUB HONOURS League Cup 2000

INTERNATIONAL HONOURS England Youth; England Under-21; England

LEICESTER'S TOP SCORER
Cottee is a dedicated professional, always looking to improve his performance. Therefore, last season the 35-year-old set himself the target of passing the previous year's tally. In fact, he was Leicester's top scorer last term with 13 Premiership goals, a terrific effort, especially as he saw Heskey depart for Liverpool in March. Although Cottee is an admirer of Heskey, the fact that he outgunned the £11m man over the season must have given him some quiet satisfaction.

TONY COTTEE

rian Deane may not have set the footballing world alight with feats of goalscoring or wizardry on the ball. But he has played at top-level football both at home and abroad for well over a decade, and at every club he has played for he has led the line superbly. With his physical presence, battling qualities – and no little amount of skill – he has proved himself a handful for defences everywhere.

Deane sets the pace

It was in his first spell at Sheffield United that Deane came to prominence. He topped the 20-goal mark in successive seasons, 1988-89 and 1989-90, and hit a total of 82 goals in his five years at Bramall Lane. His form during that period earned him an international call-up. He played three times for the senior England side, the last of them against Spain in 1993.

Deane at Elland Road

He was a Leeds United player by the time he was awarded that final cap, having moved to Elland Road in July 1993 for £2.9m, one of the biggest deals of the year. Leeds was a struggling side at the time, finishing 17th in the Premiership in the season before Deane joined the club. Eric Cantona had been sold to Manchester United and Howard Wilkinson was desperate to put a spark into the team. Deane hit 11 goals in his first season at Elland Road, and helped them to 5th place in the league. In the next three years, with Leeds in a rebuilding phase, he played 97 games and scored 21 goals.

Thrilling finale

When George Graham replaced Wilkinson in the autumn of 1996, Deane found himself surplus to requirements. He rejoined the Blades for a cut-price £1.5m, and in a short second spell with his former club he banged in 11 goals in 24 games. Graeme Souness then came to take Deane to Benfica. Souness had seen some weak performances after taking over at the famous Stadium of Light, and was keen to put some steel into the team. Enter Brian Deane, along with Scott Minto from Chelsea and Karel Poborsky from Manchester United. Deane helped the club to finish second in the Portuguese league, behind arch-rivals Porto. He scored

in a thrilling late-season 3-0 win over Porto, but it wasn't enough for Benfica to overhaul their rivals.

Robson's call

Second place was enough for a place in the expanded Champions League the following season but, with the group matches still at an early stage, Bryan Robson took 30-year-old Deane to newly promoted Middlesbrough. His first season at the Riverside produced just six goals from 26 games, but he provided an excellent foil for Hamilton Ricard, and as a strike pair they scored 21 of Boro's 48 league goals that season. It was enough to see Boro into a very respectable 9th place in the Premiership.

Productive partnership

The Deane-Ricard partnership produced 21 goals last season too, but the split was more even, with Deane hitting the net 9 times. It might have been more productive, but Boro went through a mid-season slump, when the team as a whole played badly and created very little for the front men.

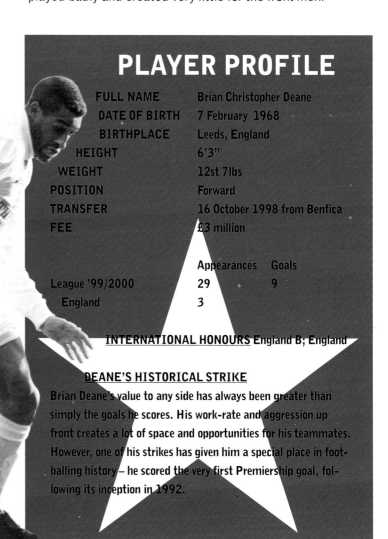

PLAYER PROFILE

FULL NAME	Brian Christopher Deane
DATE OF BIRTH	7 February 1968
BIRTHPLACE	Leeds, England
HEIGHT	6'3"
WEIGHT	12st 7lbs
POSITION	Forward
TRANSFER	16 October 1998 from Benfica
FEE	£3 million

	Appearances	Goals
League '99/2000	29	9
England	3	

INTERNATIONAL HONOURS England B; England

DEANE'S HISTORICAL STRIKE

Brian Deane's value to any side has always been greater than simply the goals he scores. His work-rate and aggression up front creates a lot of space and opportunities for his teammates. However, one of his strikes has given him a special place in footballing history – he scored the very first Premiership goal, following its inception in 1992.

BRIAN DEANE

The Celtic fans loved him, the Sheffield Wednesday fans loved him, and after just 18 months the West Ham fans have already elevated Paolo Di Canio to the status of one of the all-time great Upton Park heroes. In fact, the only person who doesn't seem to think much of the supremely gifted Di Canio is Dino Zoff, Italy's national team coach. British fans both north and south of the border have been treated to his extravagant talent in recent years, but Zoff continues to ignore a player who deserves to be seen on the biggest stages in world football.

Fiercely competitive

Di Canio isn't bitter at the way he has been overlooked; he shrugs and simply gears himself up to giving his all for his club. And Di Canio's all is really something special. He is no gifted prima donna who lets other people do the donkey work while he drifts in and out of the game. He backs up his abilities with a tremendous work rate and fierce competitiveness. He even cites training as something he particularly enjoys!

Di Canio's fiery temper

Di Canio's temperament has, of course, been his Achilles heel and got him into hot water on occasions. Most notable was the infamous incident in September 1998 when he pushed referee Paul Alcock over. Di Canio was at Sheffield Wednesday at the time, and the incident brought him a four-month ban, during which time he took himself back to Italy. Many thought that that was the last we would see of him in the Premiership, but when the ban was lifted he did return.

Fresh start

Sheffield Wed. immediately decided to offload their wayward striker, and Harry Redknapp stepped in to give the Italian a fresh start. Redknapp spoke to Tommy Burns, who had managed Di Canio at Celtic, and Burns had nothing but praise, both for his talent and his attitude.

Redknapp's shrewd deal

The fee, just £1.7m represented almost a £3m loss for Wednesday, but the club seemed pleased just to get the player off their hands. By contrast, Redknapp had sold John Hartson to Wimbledon for £7.5m. To have Di Canio on your books and the best part of £6m in your pocket had to make it one of the shrewdest deals of the season.

The top of his game

Di Canio is approaching 32 and thinks he has three years left at the top, and hopes to spend them at Upton Park. West Ham may have bought a player who was a flawed genius; now, it seems, the flaws have all disappeared.

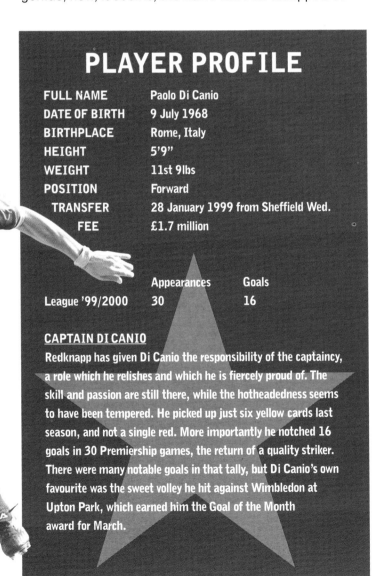

PLAYER PROFILE

FULL NAME	Paolo Di Canio
DATE OF BIRTH	9 July 1968
BIRTHPLACE	Rome, Italy
HEIGHT	5'9"
WEIGHT	11st 9lbs
POSITION	Forward
TRANSFER	28 January 1999 from Sheffield Wed.
FEE	£1.7 million

	Appearances	Goals
League '99/2000	30	16

CAPTAIN DI CANIO

Redknapp has given Di Canio the responsibility of the captaincy, a role which he relishes and which he is fiercely proud of. The skill and passion are still there, while the hotheadedness seems to have been tempered. He picked up just six yellow cards last season, and not a single red. More importantly he notched 16 goals in 30 Premiership games, the return of a quality striker. There were many notable goals in that tally, but Di Canio's own favourite was the sweet volley he hit against Wimbledon at Upton Park, which earned him the Goal of the Month award for March.

PAOLO DI CANIO

When John Gregory spent approximately half of the £12m he got for Dwight Yorke in bringing Dion Dublin to Aston Villa, he was convinced he had got an absolute bargain. The other Premiership managers obviously agreed, for the move was voted the best value transfer of the 1998-99 season.

Proven goalscorer

Gregory had acquired both a proven goalscorer and a quality centre-back at a stroke, although it was Dublin's talent as a striker that the Villa boss was most interested in. While Coventry often needed Dublin to help out at the back, Villa were already solid in that department; it was the cutting edge of the team that needed sharpening.

Explosive start

Dublin made an explosive start to his Villa career, scoring twice on his debut in a 3-2 win over Spurs, then following it up with 3 goals in a 4-1 win against Southampton and a further 2 in his third game, against Liverpool. No one could have kept up that kind of scoring rate, and Dublin has since had his barren patches, but it certainly showed why Gregory had been amazed at Coventry's willingness to let him go.

International recognition

It is not surprising that Dublin's qualities at both ends of the pitch have brought him international recognition. He was in Glenn Hoddle's squad for France '98, but was one of the unlucky group to miss out on a place in the final 22.

Manchester days

When most players leave Manchester United, it is often an indication that their best days are behind them. Dion Dublin is certainly an exception to that rule. He had gone to Old Trafford from Cambridge United in a £1m deal in August

1992, but his time there was blighted by injury. He suffered a broken leg, which put him out of action for much of the two years that he was there. He had made just 12 appearances when Alex Ferguson agreed to let him go to Coventry - although Ferguson still managed to double the money he had paid out for the Leicester-born player. In four years at Highfield Road, Dublin scored 61 League goals in 145 appearances, but his value to the team was even greater than that very creditable scoring record suggests.

Broken neck

Dublin received yet another terrible injury blow last season, this time in the shape of a broken neck. He collided with Gerald Sibon during Villa's 2-1 win against Sheffield Wednesday in December 1999, fracturing several neck vertebrae. After surgery he was expected to miss three months of the season, but his battling nature on the pitch helped with his recovery and he was back in training weeks ahead of schedule. The incentive of an FA Cup Final place no doubt played its part, too.

PLAYER PROFILE

FULL NAME	Dion Dublin
DATE OF BIRTH	22 April 1969
BIRTHPLACE	Leicester, England
HEIGHT	6'1"
WEIGHT	12st 4lbs
POSITION	Forward
TRANSFER	6 November 1998 from Coventry
FEE	£5.75 million

	Appearances	Goals
League '99/2000	26	12
England	4	

CLUB HONOURS Division Three 1991

INTERNATIONAL HONOURS England

FA CUP Dublin made a remarkable recovery from his broken neck. Only six months after the career threatening injury he lined up in the FA Cup final against Chelsea. The fairytale ending didn't materialise, however, as a lacklustre Villa failed to spark.

DION DUBLIN

Duncan Ferguson's brilliant opening strike for Newcastle United in their 3-0 win over Manchester United at St James' Park last season was notable for two reasons. First, it was a game that Alex Ferguson later singled out as an important turning point in the season, the defeat spurring his team on to the Premiership title. Second, and more important for Magpies fans, Ferguson's superbly struck volley came from a deft Shearer flick, giving an all too rare glimpse of what a fearsome duo they could be.

Dream pairing

It was Ruud Gullit who took Ferguson to St James' Park, believing that he and Shearer were a dream pairing. Unfortunately, both players were dogged by injury and they started frustratingly few games together. Gullit and Newcastle had parted company before the partnership had had the chance to really take off, and it was Bobby Robson who inherited this great potential - and frustration.

Unstoppable Ferguson

A fit Duncan Ferguson is an intimidating prospect for any defence: at times almost unstoppable in the air, but also very mobile and with good touch, considering his 6' 4" frame. An aggressive player, Big Duncan gives everything for the cause, but he has sometimes overstepped the mark, earning himself a less than perfect disciplinary record. The resulting suspensions, together with his well-documented injury problems, have sidelined the Scot too often throughout his career. But Ferguson knows only one way to play the game: full-bloodedly, and he is always liable to pick up bookings.

Ferguson the folk-hero

When he moved south from Rangers to Everton in a £4.4m deal in 1994, Ferguson settled quickly and soon became a folk-hero with the Goodison fans. He made no secret of his love for the Merseyside club. When he banged in his 37 League goals there, he invariably grabbed the badge on his shirt and kissed it in front of the fans, a gesture that many players have since taken up.

Committed and combative

He was devastated when Everton allowed him to go to Newcastle for £8m, a move that was prompted purely by financial reasons on the part of the Merseyside club. But such is 28-year-old Ferguson's committed and combative nature that he will undoubtedly continue to be a big hero on Tyneside too - provided he can stay clear of injuries.

PLAYER PROFILE

FULL NAME	Duncan Ferguson
DATE OF BIRTH	27 December 1971
BIRTHPLACE	Stirling, Scotland
HEIGHT	6'4"
WEIGHT	14st 6lbs
POSITION	Forward
TRANSFER	25 November 1998 from Everton
FEE	£8 million

	Appearances	Goals
League '99/2000	23	6
Scotland	7	

CLUB HONOURS Scottish League 1994; Scottish League Cup 1994; FA Cup 1995

INTERNATIONAL HONOURS Scotland Schoolboy; Scotland Youth; Scotland Under-21; Scotland

FERGUSON AND SCOTLAND
A long-standing rift with the Scottish FA has led to Ferguson refusing to play international football, although Scotland's coach Craig Brown has made it clear that the door is still open. As Brown's biggest headache in recent years has been a lack of firepower, he, and all Scottish fans, must be hoping that the hatchet is buried sooner rather than later.

DUNCAN FERGUSON

Chelsea are often criticised for a policy of bringing in high-profile, big-money players who are classy but perhaps past their best. Tore Andre Flo certainly can't be put into that too old, too expensive bracket. He came to Stamford Bridge as a 24-year-old in summer 1997. At the age of 27 going into the 2000-2001 season, Flo is in his prime and one of the players keeping the average age of the Chelsea squad down.

Bargain Flo

Nor was Flo one of Chelsea's expensive acquisitions. While millions were paid out on the strike-power of Zola, Laudrup, Sutton and the unlucky Pierluigi Casiraghi, the Norwegian came to Stamford Bridge for a bargain £300,000. He had been almost out of contract at SK Brann Bergen when he put himself in the shop window with a terrific display against Liverpool in a UEFA Cup tie. Joe Royle, boss at Everton at the time, had wanted to bring Flo to Goodison, but the deal fell through and it was Chelsea who snapped him up.

Flo's dribbling skills

The London club had bought themselves a tall, rangy striker who, at 6' 4", ought to be a dominant force in the air. Yet Flo's strength lies when he has the ball to feet. His control, touch and dribbling skills are prodigious for such a big man.

Twin strike

As with so many of his compatriots, Flo came to England to test himself in the competitive arena of the Premiership, and also to chase honours. Less than two years after joining the Chelsea he was part of the club's terrific cup double: the League Cup and Cup Winners' Cup victories of 1998. Flo's brilliant twin strike in the Champions' League quarter-final against Barcelona last season helped Chelsea to a superb 4-1 win. However, the disaster in the second leg at the Nou Camp, together with the team's under-achievement in the Premiership, has meant there is no Champions' League place in the coming season.

Flo's five-year contract

As a player who would be an automatic choice in most sides, Flo was initially unhappy with being in and out of the team, but now seems to have come to terms with it. He is in the middle of a five-year contract, although that hasn't prevented speculation that he might be involved in a big-money move or swap deal. It has been suggested that Chelsea's failure to earn a Champions' League spot in the coming season will prompt a big shake-up in personnel. Should Flo be a casualty of an axe-wielding Vialli, many Premiership and top European clubs will be queueing up to secure his services.

PLAYER PROFILE

FULL NAME	Tore Andre Flo
DATE OF BIRTH	15 June 1973
BIRTHPLACE	Stryn, Norway
HEIGHT	6'4"
WEIGHT	13st 8lbs
POSITION	Forward
TRANSFER	4 August 1997 from SK Brann Bergen
FEE	£300,000

	Appearances	Goals
League '99/2000	33	10
Norway	44	

CLUB HONOURS League Cup 1998; European Cup Winners Cup 1998; Super Cup 1998; FA Cup 2000.

INTERNATIONAL HONOURS Norway

MAKING AN IMPACT
Throughout his time at Stamford Bridge, Flo has been one of the biggest casualties of Chelsea's much-publicised squad rotation policy. On many occasions a top performance one week has still left him on the bench the next. Unfortunately for Flo, Vialli has said that he believes the Norwegian is the best in the business at coming off the bench to make an impact, rather than starting games - the dreaded 'Supersub' tag.

TORE ANDRE FLO

When pressed on the subject of the most memorable goal he had scored, Robbie Fowler nominated two from the same match - one a header and the other a volley, in the FA Cup semi-final win over Aston Villa in 1996. But it is the fact that he had to be pushed to single out any particular goal that is more significant. Fowler's view is that of all great strikers: 'A goal is a goal, whether you score from one yard or 25 yards.'

The clinical finisher

Since his debut for Liverpool as an 18-year-old in September 1993, Fowler has scored his share of spectacular goals. But it is the reputation he has built up as the most clinical finisher in the business that undoubtedly gives him more pleasure. The striker's art is all about converting chances into goals, and by that yardstick Fowler is a class apart.

Natural successor

Fowler showed what he could do in that very first match, a League Cup tie against Fulham. He scored in the away leg - then got all five goals in a 5-0 win at Anfield in the return match. He went on to fire a highly creditable 18 goals in that 1993-94 season, but it was during the following three years that he hit top gear. He passed the 30-goal mark in all competitions in each of those campaigns, firmly establishing himself as the natural successor to the great Ian Rush.

Fowler's first international

With that kind of scoring form, international recognition was inevitable. Terry Venables handed him his first England cap in 1996, when he came on as substitute against Bulgaria. Later that same year he got his first international start, in a match against Croatia.

Back to his best

Fowler looked on course to rewrite the goalscoring record books. But in February

1998, he suffered a bad knee injury in a match against Everton, the team he had supported as a boy. It happened as a result of a clash with Everton 'keeper Thomas Myhre, and kept him out for seven months. When he did return to action, several weeks ahead of schedule, he soon showed that he had lost none of his sharpness in front of goal.

150 goals for Liverpool

Fowler was made vice-captain, and the 1999-2000 season started well. He scored in the opening game, a 2-1 win over Sheffield Wednesday, and followed it up with a great strike against Arsenal at Anfield. But injury struck him down again, this time an ankle problem that needed two operations. One bright spot in another frustrating season was the header he got in Liverpool's 3-1 win over Wimbledon during the Christmas period. It marked his 150th goal for the club. A goal every two games is the record of a quality forward; Fowler's strike rate is significantly better than that.

PLAYER PROFILE

FULL NAME	Robert Bernard Fowler
DATE OF BIRTH	9 April 1975
BIRTHPLACE	Liverpool, England
HEIGHT	5'11"
WEIGHT	11st 10lbs
POSITION	Forward
TRANSFER	Signed as trainee

	Appearances	Goals
League '99/2000	14	3
England	11	2

CLUB HONOURS League Cup 1995

INTERNATIONAL HONOURS England Youth (UEFA YC 1993); England Under-21; England B; England

FOWLER'S FUTURE
During the 1998-99 season Fowler became involved in a protracted dispute with Liverpool over a new contract. Rumours began to circulate that he might be on his way out of Anfield. Arsene Wenger headed a long queue of admirers of Fowler's ability. But the player finally settled his differences with Liverpool, signed a new contract and committed himself to the club he loves.

ROBBIE FOWLER

There are few better sights in football than Ryan Giggs in full flight. The modern game is all about pace, and when Giggs is on one of his lightning bursts, he takes some catching. Defenders try everything - diving in, backing off, doubling up - but when Giggs is on song, his balance and tight control are so good that it is extremely hard to get the ball off him.

Talented teenager

Giggs was born in Wales but moved to England at the age of seven. With his Welsh roots and his attacking flair, it's hardly surprising that his childhood heroes were Mark Hughes and Ian Rush. Both Manchester clubs were aware of the talented young teenager on their doorstep, but City showed no interest in pursuing him. Alex Ferguson signed him on schoolboy forms as soon as he turned fourteen, and he joined the professional ranks almost exactly three years later.

Fabulous derby debut

Ferguson gave the 17-year-old his full debut by throwing him into the cauldron of a derby match against City in May 1991. Giggs marked the occasion by scoring the only goal of the match. He thus became the first in what has since become a production line of gifted young players. Of the present United squad, the only other survivor from that era is Denis Irwin.

Giggs's immense talent

If there has been a weakness in Giggs's game, it's been in the delivery of the final ball. Also, for such an immense talent, some feel he should get on the scoresheet more often. Last season's campaign brought him just six goals from 30 games. But whether he is scoring or not, many feel that Giggs brings something extra to the team, in much the same way that Bergkamp seems to make Arsenal tick.

Comparisons with the greatest

Giggs is the youngest ever Welsh international. But over the years Welsh supporters have been frustrated by the number of times that he has pulled out of international squads through injury. In chasing honours, realistically, Giggs must look to club rather than country. In that respect he is in a similar position

to the player he was inevitably compared with in the early days - George Best. With six Premiership titles, three FA Cup wins, and now that European Cup winners' medal, Giggs comfortably exceeds Best's haul - and he is still only 26.

Best and Giggs

Alex Ferguson is quick to dismiss any comparisons between Best and Giggs. Best was a unique talent. But then, so is Giggs.

PLAYER PROFILE

FULL NAME	Ryan Joseph Giggs
DATE OF BIRTH	29 November 1973
BIRTHPLACE	Cardiff, Wales
HEIGHT	5'11"
WEIGHT	10st 9lbs
POSITION	Midfielder
TRANSFER	Signed as trainee

	Appearances	Goals
League '99/2000	30	6
Wales	24	

CLUB HONOURS European Super Cup 1991; FA Youth Cup 1992; League Cup 1992; Premier League 1993, 1994, 1996, 1997, 1999, 2000; Charity Shield 1993, 1994, 1996, 1997; FA Cup 1994, 1996, 1999; European Cup 1999

INTERNATIONAL HONOURS England Schoolboy; Wales Youth; Wales Under-21; Wales

SENSATIONAL SOLO EFFORT
When Giggs does score, it's very often one for the scrapbook. The solo effort which beat arch-rivals Arsenal in the FA Cup semi-final replay in 1999 was vintage Giggs. Picking the ball up wide on the left near the halfway line, the threat looked harmless enough. Giggs then proceeded to dance and shimmy his way through the entire Arsenal defence before thundering the ball into the roof of the net. There were similarities between this and David Ginola's terrific individual goal against Barnsley, also in the Cup the same year. But for carving his way through the meanest defence of the last decade, Giggs's strike must have the edge.

RYAN GIGGS

A world-beater when your team's got the ball; doesn't do enough when the opposition is in possession. This just about sums up a manager's conundrum where David Ginola is concerned. Fans love his sublime skills, but in the modern game, where coaches pore over systems and formations, talent alone doesn't seem to be enough. Defenders have to be comfortable going forward and attacking players are also required to track back.

Flair and style

When Ginola was part of the attacking side Kevin Keegan built at Newcastle United, he seemed perfectly at home. The philosophy was regarded as kamikaze football by some, but Ginola revelled in a team which believed an open, entertaining 4-3 win was much better than playing defensively and grinding out a 1-0 result. For their part, the Toon Army loved the flair and style Ginola brought to the side.

Player of the Year

In 1997, Christian Gross took the Frenchman to Tottenham, another club with a long and proud tradition of playing scintillating, attacking football. Unfortunately, Spurs were struggling at the time, Gross was soon gone and George Graham was brought in to turn things around. The pundits immediately began predicting that Graham would sacrifice his 'luxury' player in an effort to put more steel into the side and make them harder to beat. The new Spurs boss defied the odds, however, openly declaring his admiration for Ginola's ability. Ginola responded by weaving his magic, week in and week out during the 1998-99 season. He won both Player of the Year awards, edging out all the candidates from the treble-winning Manchester United side.

Ginola's wizardry

Picking out examples of Ginola's wizardry is no easy task, but the way he took on the whole of the Barnsley defence before slotting the ball home in an FA Cup tie stands out in the memory. Although Ginola has scored many breathtaking solo goals, an appreciation of his game has to take into account the number of assists he can take credit for - often pin-point crosses after tying full-backs in knots.

Ginola's future

Last season saw Spurs still languishing in mid-table, with Ginola substituted on many occasions. Then, at the end of the season, he was left out of the side completely when Spurs visited Old Trafford. This raised the issue of Ginola's future all over again. Ginola has said that he regrets not having played for one of the top clubs in Europe. Many people will feel that his silky skills ought to have graced the biggest stages in both club and international football.

PLAYER PROFILE

FULL NAME	David Ginola
DATE OF BIRTH	25 January 1967
BIRTHPLACE	Gassin, France
HEIGHT	6'0"
WEIGHT	11st 10lbs
POSITION	Forward
TRANSFER	18 July 1997 from Newcastle
FEE	£2 million

	Appearances	Goals
League '99/2000	36	4
France	17	

AWARDS French Player of the Year 1994; Players' Player of the Year 1994; Football Writers Footballer of the Year 1999; PFA Player of the Year 1999

CLUB HONOURS French Cup 1993, 1994, 1995; French League Cup 1995; League Cup 1999

INTERNATIONAL HONOURS France

GINOLA AND FRANCE It is ironic that while Ginola was receiving accolades for his performances for Spurs, he was merely commentating for TV as his compatriots became World Cup winners. Ginola has not played for France since a World Cup qualifier against Bulgaria in 1993. Liverpool manager Gerard Houllier was in charge of the national side at the time, and he blamed Ginola for the goal that cost France a place in the finals at USA '94.

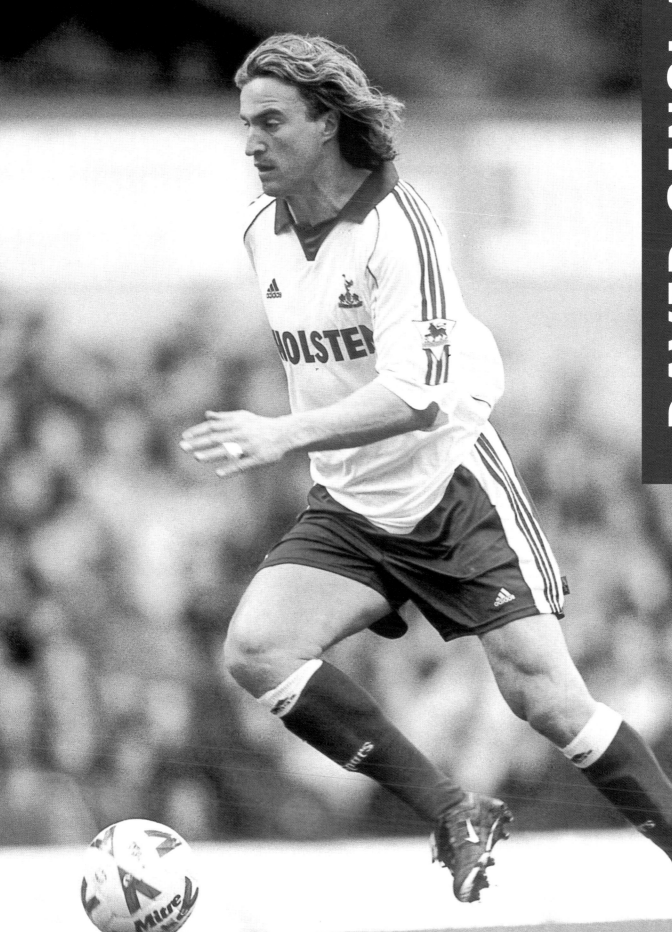

DAVID GINOLA

I t has taken Shaun Goater a long time to become an overnight success. Manchester City's hitman will soon be in the spotlight, testing himself against the best defences. But 30-year-old Goater has waited a long time for the chance to show what he can do at the top level. It has been a journey that has lasted more than a decade, time he has spent in the lower leagues learning his trade.

Bermuda to Old Trafford

Goater's story began in Manchester, too, but on the red side of the city rather than the blue. He left his Bermuda home for Old Trafford in 1988. United had been visiting the island on a mid-season break, when 18-year-old Goater lined up against them for a local side. He impressed enough to be invited over for a trial, and that led to the offer of a contract.

Improving player

The dream then went slightly sour. Goater spent 18 months at United, waiting for his chance. It never came, and he was offered out to Rotherham on loan. He ended up spending six years at Millmoor, a move he now regards as an important stepping-stone on the way to improving himself as a player.

Goater's strike rate

His 70 League goals for Rotherham caught the eye of Joe Jordan, manager of Bristol City, and Goater moved to Ashton Gate in 1996 for £175,000. His strike rate was already very respectable, but in less than two seasons at Bristol it improved dramatically. He netted 40 goals from just 67 starts, plus eight substitute appearances.

Relegation battle

In March 1998, Goater was nearly out of contract, and Bristol agreed to sell him to Manchester City for £400,000, just before the transfer deadline. Joe Royle's side were in a dogfight at the wrong end of the table and he was desperate to add some firepower in a bid to avoid relegation. The bid failed, and City suffered the ignominy of dropping down to Division Two at the end of the 1997-98

season. On a personal note, however, Goater's three goals in seven games showed that he was the man for the job.

Goater and City bounce back

The last two seasons have seen back-to-back promotion campaigns at Maine Road. Goater led the line and scored 21 goals as City bounced straight back up to the Division One; then, last season, he banged in 29 in all competitions, making him not only City's top scorer, but the overall hotshot in that very competitive league.

Accuracy over power

One thing in Goater's favour is that although he is strong and quick, he favours accuracy over power. He likes to pass the ball into the net, rather than blast it. If he manages to pass one into the back of Manchester United's net this season, it will be a truly amazing turn in the wheel of fortune for Shaun Goater.

PLAYER PROFILE

FULL NAME	Leonard Shaun Goater
DATE OF BIRTH	25 February 1970
BIRTHPLACE	Hamilton, Bermuda
HEIGHT	6'1"
WEIGHT	12st 0lbs
POSITION	Forward
TRANSFER	26 March 1998 from Bristol City
FEE	£400,000

	Appearances	Goals
Div One '99/2000	39	23
Bermuda	9	

CLUB HONOURS Associated Members' Cup 1996

INTERNATIONAL HONOURS Bermuda

GOATER'S NEW CHALLENGE
Goater has averaged a goal every two games over the past four years. He will be doing brilliantly if he gets anywhere near that figure playing against Premiership defences. But he will relish the challenge. Goater has spent his career proving the doubters wrong - and that includes winning over the City fans who didn't think he was good enough for the First Division.

SHAUN GOATER

When Thierry Henry climbed brilliantly to meet Ray Parlour's cross and power his header towards the Galatasaray goal, it came mightily close to capping an unbelievable first season at Arsenal. As it was, Taffarel in the Galatasaray goal pulled off a super save, Arsenal lost the UEFA Cup on penalties - and Henry had to be content with a fabulous goal-rush which made him the Premiership's top striker in the back half of the season.

16 league goals in 19 games

The statistics may not tell the whole story, but they are truly remarkable, nevertheless. Henry's haul for the season was a very creditable 17 league goals. But when it is remembered that he netted just once in his first 12 Premiership starts, it shows what devastating form he was in from December onwards. It brought him 16 goals in 19 games, and prior to that disappointing Copenhagen final, he notched 7 goals in 7 games in the UEFA Cup for good measure.

Henry's impact

Arsenal fans must be especially pleased with the impact Henry has made, following the antics of his predecessor as Highbury's Top Gunner - Nicolas Anelka. At the beginning of last season they must have thought that they would miss Anelka's goals, if not Anelka himself. But Arsene Wenger has not only replaced Anelka's goalscoring prowess, he has done it at less than half the price. On top of that, he handed over to Real Madrid all the disruptive tantrums that Anelka brings with him.

Top sprinter

"Titi" Henry was a top sprinter as a youngster, and the combination of his athleticism and ball skills was bound to get him noticed, and it did - by none other than Arsene Wenger! Wenger was Monaco's coach when he had Henry first time round, handing him his debut as a 17-year-old.

Winger to striker

Henry was a terrific wide player, but in the central role that Wenger has asked him to play he has been an absolute revelation. The Arsenal boss saw he had the potential to play in that position - even before the player himself, who didn't think his finishing would be good enough. Now, however, Henry is relishing the role, and recognises how much he has come on as a player over the past year. He puts this improvement down to the quality of his Arsenal team-mates, and of course, Arsene Wenger.

Midas Touch

Having picked up Anelka for a song, sold him for £20m-plus and brought in Thierry Henry for £11m, it must go down as the latest example of Wenger's Midas Touch in the transfer market.

PLAYER PROFILE

FULL NAME	Thierry Henry
DATE OF BIRTH	17 August 1977
BIRTHPLACE	Paris, France
HEIGHT	6'1"
WEIGHT	12st 2lbs
POSITION	Forward
TRANSFER	3 August 1999 from Juventus
FEE	£11 million

	Appearances	Goals
League '99/2000	31	17

INTERNATIONAL HONOURS France

WORLD CUP TRIUMPH

It was during France's glorious World Cup triumph in 1998 that Henry emerged as a major talent. France had gone into the tournament in a state of uncertainty regarding the striking department. Christophe Dugarry and Stephane Guivarc'h were not in great form, while the young Anelka was promising but untried and raw. Enter Thierry Henry, who contributed 3 goals in France's group matches, making him their top scorer. He didn't play in the final, though, which he naturally regards as his biggest disappointment to date.

THIERRY HENRY

Emile Ivanhoe Heskey's £11m move from Leicester City to Liverpool in March of this year was just about the worst-kept secret in football. Speculation about Heskey's future was so intense in the months leading up to the move that it only appeared to be a question of timing. Right up until the deal was done Leicester boss Martin O'Neill signalled his hope that 'Bruno' would remain at Filbert Street. But as the news broke, not even Leicester fans seemed very surprised.

Leicester's boy

Heskey went to the same school as another famous Leicester player who went on to bigger and better things with a Merseyside club - Gary Lineker. The Leicester City of today - a team that consistently finishes in the top half of the Premiership, not to mention one that has a cup-winning pedigree - is a far stronger outfit than the one Lineker left. But Liverpool are one of the elite, and Heskey will be hoping that the quality players around him there, and the service that they will give him, will make him a better player.

Prodigious talent

From Gerard Houllier's point of view, £11m is a lot to pay for a player who is nowhere near the finished article. But the Anfield boss will be hoping to see the blossoming of Heskey's prodigious talent. He tracked Heskey's career over a considerable period and obviously sees him as another piece of the jigsaw, the completion of which will hopefully see Liverpool mount a serious title challenge.

Front-line power

There will be several permutations in the striking department for Houllier to consider, but Heskey and Owen looks an interesting prospect. The two know each other well, having starred together for the England Under-18 side that finished 3rd in the European Championships in France. With Camara, Meijer and Robbie Fowler on the scene, though, Houllier will have his work cut out keeping everyone happy. Indeed, Heskey's arrival at Anfield once again sparked off talk that Fowler might be allowed to leave.

Heskey's pace and power

Heskey has a formidable combination of power and pace in his 6ft 2in frame, but his Achilles heel has been his goal return. He had netted just 6 Premiership goals all season when Liverpool signed him, and an overall record of one goal every five games is poor when compared, for example, with Fowler's.

Immediate impact

Heskey didn't take long to make his presence felt at his new club, however. Just two days and a single training session after the deal was completed, he pulled on a Liverpool shirt in a match against Sunderland. After only three minutes he made a surging run into the box, went down under a challenge and won his side a penalty.

PLAYER PROFILE

FULL NAME	Emile William Ivanhoe Heskey
DATE OF BIRTH	11 January 1978
BIRTHPLACE	Leicester, England
HEIGHT	6'2"
WEIGHT	13st 12lbs
POSITION	Forward
TRANSFER	10 March 2000 from Leicester
FEE	£11 million

	Appearances	Goals
League '99/2000	35	10
England	6	1

CLUB HONOURS League Cup 1997, 2000

INTERNATIONAL HONOURS England Youth; England Under-21; England B International; England

HESKEY'S INTERNATIONAL FUTURE
Like Gerard Houllier, England manager Kevin Keegan sees terrific potential in Heskey. He handed the player his first senior cap on February 22 this year. Intriguingly, with Alan Shearer having announced his retirement from international football after Euro 2000, some pundits believe Keegan will look to the Heskey-Owen combination to spearhead England's assault on the World Cup in 2002.

EMILE HESKEY

The manager of Stockport County, Andy Kilner, was magnanimous in defeat: "That's what you get with quality strikers. He had three chances and took them all. He was the difference between the sides." The player he was referring to was Andy Hunt. Kilner had just watched his side play terrifically, yet go down 3-1 to Charlton in last season's Division One clash at Edgeley Park. Stockport had dominated the game early on and gone 1-0 up against the league leaders. Andy Hunt then proceeded to score a brilliant hat-trick which knocked the stuffing out of them. In fact, Hunt knocked Stockport for six – quite literally –for he had also hit three against them at the game at The Valley earlier in the season.

Hunt's fabulous season

Hunt's manager Alan Curbishley saw the Stockport game as typical of the season as a whole: chances falling to Hunt and Hunt putting them away with monotonous regularity.

Andy's 25 goals

He went on to notch 25 goals for Charlton in their brilliant championship-winning campaign last season. 24 of them were in the league; the other was the last-minute winner in the team's terrific 3-2 win against Coventry at Highfield Road in the FA Cup. Not bad for a player who cost Charlton precisely nothing. When he signed for the club in the summer of 1998, he became their first acquisition under the Bosman ruling.

Hunt's early career

Hunt began his career at non-league Kettering, before joining Newcastle in a £150,000 deal in January 1991. After two years on Tyneside, he went to West Bromwich Albion for a bargain £100,000. He was a great servant at the Hawthorns, hitting 85 goals in his five years at the club.

Playing against the best

Hunt joined Charlton just after the club had secured Premiership status, following their dramatic play-off victory over Sunderland. That first taste of playing against the elite, in the 1998-99 season, ultimately ended in relegation. Hunt partnered Clive Mendonca up front for the most part, and came in for some criticism during that unhappy Premiership baptism. He held the ball up well and won his share of aerial battles, but struggled to find the net. He scored both goals in a 2-2 draw against Spurs at White Hart Lane, but that proved to be the highlight and he finished the season with just seven goals. With that kind of a return from a main striker, it was always going to be difficult for the club to survive.

The new season

Alan Curbishley will be looking to emulate Sunderland, who did superbly second time around in the top division. They did have a certain Kevin Phillips to bang in the goals, though, and therein lies the key. Promoted sides are invariably hard-working and well-organised, but tend to struggle in the goalscoring department. So it's a fair bet that Andy Hunt will have to do considerably better than seven Premiership goals this time round if Charlton are to survive.

PLAYER PROFILE

FULL NAME	Andrew Hunt
DATE OF BIRTH	9 June 1970
BIRTHPLACE	Thurrock, England
HEIGHT	6'0"
WEIGHT	12st 0lbs
POSITION	Forward
TRANSFER	2 July 1998 from West Bromwich Albion
FEE	Free

	Appearances	Goals
Div One '99/2000	44	24

HUNT'S EXPERIENCE

Last season, back in Division One, Hunt answered his critics by turning in classy forward displays week after week. He will be keen to take that form into the new season and his second crack at Premiership defences. The experience of two years ago should help enormously.

STEFFEN IVERSEN　　TOTTENHAM HOTSPUR & NORWAY

Steffen Iversen hasn't enjoyed the greatest good fortune since his arrival at Spurs as a 20-year-old in December 1996. He has not only seen the departure of the manager who bought him from Rosenborg, Gerry Francis, but he has also watched Christian Gross come and go. Now, under George Graham, Tottenham are in a rebuilding phase. Graham wants to create a side capable of challenging for the top honours. Although Iversen will surely be part of the Spurs boss's long-term plans, players coming and going won't make the striker's task any easier.

Sidelined by injury

Iversen has also been badly hit by injuries in his time at the club. He missed most of the 1997-98 season, and has been sidelined by a number of minor knocks besides. Fellow strikers Les Ferdinand and Chris Armstrong have also been unfortunate in that respect, and that has made it difficult for Iversen to form a settled attacking partnership.

Firing Spurs to Wembley

The last 18 months have looked brighter for the Norwegian international, though. At the back end of the 1998-99 season, he scored the goal which took Spurs to Wembley for the first time in eight years. It was a lovely 25-yard chip in a Worthington Cup semi-final against Wimbledon at Selhurst Park.

14-goal haul

Last season he missed just two Premiership games, and his 14 goals was the 8th best tally in the division. His haul included a hat-trick in Spurs' memorable 7-2 mauling of Southampton at White Hart Lane in March.

Terrific athlete

Iversen is a terrific athlete, powerful but very agile for a six-footer. He is also quick and tenacious and doesn't give defenders time to settle. Like compatriot Tore Andre Flo,

he has good touch for such a big man. With Ole Gunnar Solskjaer also available to the Norwegian coach, it is no wonder that the country has been such a formidable attacking side in recent years.

Powerful shot

Iversen may not have the clinical finishing skills of the Baby-faced Assassin yet, but with the right kind of service he is a handful for any defence. He is an intelligent player who makes good runs, and when he gets a sniff of the target he needs no second invitation to unleash his powerful shot.

PLAYER PROFILE

FULL NAME	Steffen Iversen
DATE OF BIRTH	10 November 1976
BIRTHPLACE	Oslo, Norway
HEIGHT	6'1"
WEIGHT	11st 10lbs
POSITION	Forward
TRANSFER	7 December 1996 from Rosenborg
FEE	£2.7 million

	Appearances	Goals
League '99/2000	36	14

CLUB HONOURS
League Cup 1999

INTERNATIONAL HONOURS
Norway Youth, Norway Under-21; Norwegian League Championship 1995, 1996; Norwegian Cup 1995

IVERSEN'S FUTURE
Top strikers will look to score 20 goals in a season. That is the kind of return Teddy Sheringham managed over five glorious years at White Hart Lane. Iversen, who was brought in to replace Sheringham, hasn't fulfilled his promise yet. But if he should stay clear of injuries, there is still plenty of time for him to put himself up there in the White Hart Lane hall of fame.

STEFFEN IVERSEN

Francis Jeffers became something of an overnight sensation during the latter part of the 1998-99 season. The former trainee found himself catapulted into the limelight at a time when Everton were struggling and desperate for points. There was no gentle introduction to the demands of Premiership football. It was a case of "if you're good enough, you're old enough", and Walter Smith had no hesitation in throwing the talented youngster into the cauldron of a relegation battle.

16-year-old debut

It was all a far cry from the season before, when Jeffers made just a single appearance as a substitute. That came in a defeat against Manchester United, but at least Jeffers had the consolation of becoming only the second 16-year-old in the club's history to figure in a first-team match.

Jeffers off the mark

Jeffers had just turned 18 when he was handed his full Premiership debut, and from that moment the acclaim and recognition came thick and fast. And the goals. He very nearly opened his account for Everton in that debut match, against Derby at Pride Park, but Nick Barmby took the ball off his toes. That first goal wasn't long in coming, though. He got on the scoresheet just a week later, in his home debut. He went on to finish the season with 7 goals, second only to Kevin Campbell. The ex-Arsenal man only arrived at Goodison in March, on loan from Trabzonspor. The pair struck up a terrific understanding, and the goals flew in from all angles. Everton had had a lean spell in front of goal, but now the floodgates opened. Confidence in the strikers bred confidence throughout the team, and Walter Smith's side not only staved off relegation, but looked a very promising outfit for the future.

Rave reviews

The experienced Campbell might have been the senior partner, but the pundits enthused over the quality and maturity in Jeffers's performances. There may have been quicker players over the ground, but he more than

made up for it with the intelligence and timing of his runs. Add that to his excellent tight control and instinctive eye for goal and it is no wonder that he started getting rave reviews. Last season proved to be something of an anti-climax for Jeffers. After his earlier achievements, expectations were much higher as the season got under way. Jeffers himself wanted it to be the year in which he really established himself as a Premiership striker. It started well enough, with goals in consecutive Premiership games against Southampton and Wimbledon in August. Then, in September, he scored on his debut for the England Under-21 side against Luxembourg. But the season went downhill from there. Injuries meant that from the beginning of October to the middle of April he played just eight Premiership games.

Star for the future

Overall, it was a season Jeffers will be happy to forget. This emerging talent may have been prevented from really breaking through last term, but he looks a cast-iron certainty to be a star for both club and country for many years to come.

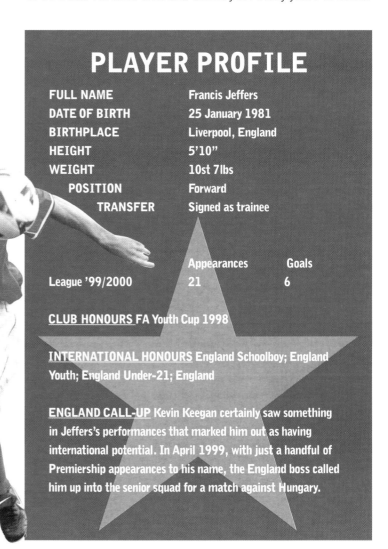

PLAYER PROFILE

FULL NAME	Francis Jeffers
DATE OF BIRTH	25 January 1981
BIRTHPLACE	Liverpool, England
HEIGHT	5'10"
WEIGHT	10st 7lbs
POSITION	Forward
TRANSFER	Signed as trainee

	Appearances	Goals
League '99/2000	21	6

CLUB HONOURS FA Youth Cup 1998

INTERNATIONAL HONOURS England Schoolboy; England Youth; England Under-21; England

ENGLAND CALL-UP Kevin Keegan certainly saw something in Jeffers's performances that marked him out as having international potential. In April 1999, with just a handful of Premiership appearances to his name, the England boss called him up into the senior squad for a match against Hungary.

FRANCIS JEFFERS

When 21-year-old Julian Joachim left Leicester City for Aston Villa in 1996, he was following in the footsteps of illustrious strikers such as Gary Lineker and Alan Smith, who had moved on from Filbert Street to further their ambitions. Joachim was one of the brightest young talents in the country when he was at Leicester, having joined the club as a trainee at the age of 17. His four years at Filbert Street may have yielded just one goal every four League games, but he was widely regarded as a player with a big future.

Joachim's pace

It was Brian Little who stepped in to give Joachim his chance in the top flight. Little knew all about his pace and trickery, having been his manager at Leicester. When Little moved to Villa Park, it wasn't long before Joachim followed.

Striking competition

He initially found his chances limited. Dwight Yorke and Savo Milosevic were at the club; then, barely a year after Joachim joined Villa, Stan Collymore arrived from Liverpool with a hefty £7m price tag. Villa's most expensive acquisition pushed Joachim even further down the pecking order in the striking department.

Unsettling times

In 1997-98, Collymore's first full season at the club, Joachim equalled Stan the Man's haul of 8 goals. The form of both Collymore and Milosevic was erratic, and both became increasingly unsettled. Dwight Yorke was unsettled, too, and it became clear that he wanted away from Villa Park.

Top scorer

All three players eventually left, and Little also parted company with the club. New boss John Gregory brought in Paul Merson as the 1998-99 season got under way, with Dion Dublin joining shortly afterwards. Joachim hit it off straight away with Dublin. It was a classic "little and large" partnership, and with Merson providing the guile and creativity just behind them, Villa had a cutting edge which helped them set the early Premiership pace. Joachim enjoyed his best spell at the club. He was rarely out of the side and finished the season as top scorer.

Fluctuating form

Last season was an up-and-down affair, both for Joachim and the team. He featured in 33 of Villa's League games, but played the full 90 minutes in just about half of them and scored only six times. There were no FA Cup goals for Joachim, either, while Benito Carbone hit five on Villa's run that took them to Wembley. It was the Italian who got the nod alongside Dublin for the final against Chelsea, Joachim having to settle for a place on the bench.

PLAYER PROFILE

FULL NAME	Julian Kevin Joachim
DATE OF BIRTH	20 September 1974
BIRTHPLACE	Boston
HEIGHT	5'6"
WEIGHT	12st 2lbs
POSITION	Forward
TRANSFER	24 February 1996 from Leicester
FEE	£1.5 million

	Appearances	Goals
League '99/2000	33	6

INTERNATIONAL HONOURS England Youth (UEFAC 1993); England Under-21

JOACHIM'S ENGLAND AMBITIONS
At 25 there is still time for Joachim to fulfil the promise he showed as a teenager. But if he has ambitions to build on the England Under-21 honours he has achieved, he needs to bang in the goals more consistently and make it impossible for Gregory to leave him out of the Villa side.

It is often said that football today may be fast and skilful, but there just aren't enough characters in the game. Fans love individual, unpredictable players, those who can bring crowds to their feet with blinding flashes of skill - and turn games in the process. Players like Nwankwo Kanu. Kanu's flair and inventiveness have been a breath of fresh air in the Premiership. All football fans - not just Gooners - like the fact that he is always looking to try something different. His flicks and tricks may not always come off, but when they do, he is a joy to watch.

Memorable hat-trick

Flair players, by their very nature, drift in and out of games. The statistics for last season's Premiership campaign suggest that Kanu does most of his damage in short bursts. He played in 15 full Premiership games for Arsenal last season, but scored in only one of them - that memorable hat-trick he grabbed against Chelsea at Stamford Bridge, turning a 2-0 deficit into a 3-2 victory. On the other hand, in the 16 games where he didn't play the full 90 minutes, Kanu found the net 9 times.

Heart problems

He first made a name for himself when he helped Ajax to win the Champions' League final against AC Milan in 1995. He then moved to Italy, joining Inter Milan, but before he had much of a chance to show what he could do in Serie A, he received some devastating news. Doctors informed him that he had a heart problem which not only threatened his career, but also his life. He underwent surgery and was out of action for a year, but vowed to fight his way back to full fitness.

Wenger's 5 million pound bargain

Unfortunately, when he did recover, he found himself the forgotten man at Inter and the Italian club was quite prepared to let him go. Arsène Wenger stepped in to revitalise his career, paying £5m for his services early in 1999.

Kanu the showman

With his languid style, loping stride and those enormous size 14 boots, Kanu quickly made himself one of the characters and showmen of the Premiership. For his goal celebration he does a sharpshooter display to the crowd which is pure entertainment. He may look unorthodox and ungainly, but he has considerable technical ability and plenty of tricks up his sleeve. Defenders find him a very awkward customer to mark.

Kanu's magic

"Boring, boring Arsenal" used to be a regular cry among football fans. Kanu's highly individual brand of magic has helped make the Gunners one of the most entertaining sides in the country.

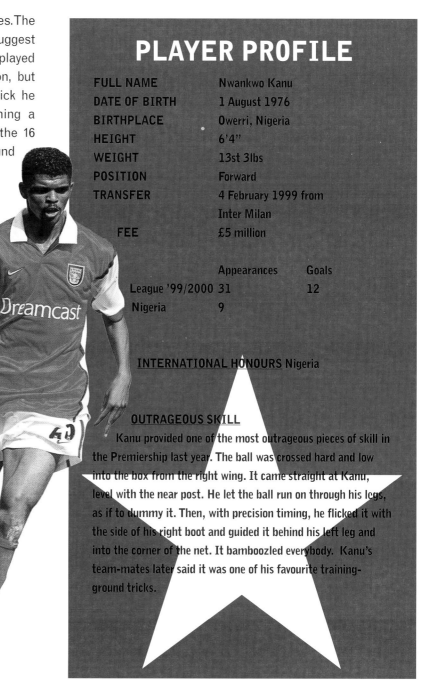

PLAYER PROFILE

FULL NAME	Nwankwo Kanu
DATE OF BIRTH	1 August 1976
BIRTHPLACE	Owerri, Nigeria
HEIGHT	6'4"
WEIGHT	13st 3lbs
POSITION	Forward
TRANSFER	4 February 1999 from Inter Milan
FEE	£5 million

	Appearances	Goals
League '99/2000	31	12
Nigeria	9	

INTERNATIONAL HONOURS Nigeria

OUTRAGEOUS SKILL

Kanu provided one of the most outrageous pieces of skill in the Premiership last year. The ball was crossed hard and low into the box from the right wing. It came straight at Kanu, level with the near post. He let the ball run on through his legs, as if to dummy it. Then, with precision timing, he flicked it with the side of his right boot and guided it behind his left leg and into the corner of the net. It bamboozled everybody. Kanu's team-mates later said it was one of his favourite training-ground tricks.

NWANKWO KANU

ROBBIE KEANE

COVENTRY CITY & EIRE

When a player shines in lower-league football, there are always talent-spotters from the Premiership watching and wondering if he has what it takes to make it at a higher level. Top clubs will often take a chance on a player with potential - as long as the price is right. The problem today is the soaring inflation that has occurred in transfer fees. When a Division One side slaps a multi-million-pound valuation on a player, then the top clubs will inevitably be more cautious.

Hot property

Robbie Keane is a classic case of this relatively recent phenomenon. The Dublin-born teenager was undoubtedly the hottest property in Division One. By the time he was 17, he was not only established in Wolves' first team, but he was their top scorer for the 1997-98 season. He was also a Republic of Ireland international.

Robbie's choice of clubs

This rise to prominence justified Keane's decision to go to Molineux. When he was a youngster playing for Crumlin, he had the chance to join Liverpool, but he felt that opportunities to play first-team football would be greater at Wolves. By the end of the 1998-99 season, however, Keane was ready to make the step up in class, and Wolves were ready to cash in and let him go.

Transfer madness

The club naturally wanted big money for their top young player. But when a figure of £5m was mentioned, many respected figures in the game thought it was absolute madness. Most notable among these was Sir Alex Ferguson himself, who said that a figure of £500,000 would be more realistic. He added fuel to the debate by suggesting that Keane would struggle to get into the Manchester United reserve team.

Keane interest

In spite of such remarks, several top clubs expressed an interest in Keane, with Aston Villa appearing to be the front runners. John Gregory was still interested at £5m, but when the price hit the £6m mark, the Villa boss thought enough was enough and withdrew from the race, far from pleased.

Outstanding debut

Both Coventry and Middlesbrough were prepared to meet the asking price, but Keane chose to stay in the Midlands and went to Highfield Road. He made his debut in a home match against Derby on the first day of last season. All eyes were on him, looking to see if Gordon Strachan had wasted his money or made a shrewd investment. Keane turned in an outstanding performance, scoring both goals in a 2-0 win. Strachan brought him off with five minutes to go so that he could take his much-deserved applause from the Highfield Road crowd.

Keane silences the doubters

He went on to hit 12 goals from his 31 League appearances last term. In the process he silenced all the doubters, not only with his goals, but with his speed of thought and movement, combined with great balance and footwork. He also works hard for the team and is very competitive.

PLAYER PROFILE

FULL NAME	Robert David Keane
DATE OF BIRTH	8 July 1980
BIRTHPLACE	Dublin, Eire
HEIGHT	5'9"
WEIGHT	11st 10lbs
POSITION	Forward
TRANSFER	19 August 1999 from Wolverhampton Wanderers
FEE	£6 million

	Appearances	Goals
League '99/2000	31	12
Eire	9	

INTERNATIONAL HONOURS Eire B International; Eire

SIX-MILLION-POUND STEAL Robbie Keane will turn 20 as the new season gets under way. For such quality at such a young age, £6m is starting to look like an absolute steal. As for Coventry fans, having seen the likes of Dublin and Huckerby leave, they will enjoy having one of the most exciting young attacking players in the country at Highfield Road.

ROBBIE KEANE

oward Wilkinson has said that developing young talent not only has the obvious benefit of saving a fortune in the transfer market, but also gives players a greater sense of belonging to a club. When Wilkinson was manager of Leeds United, he set up a much-admired youth system which is now bearing fruit. One of the most exciting talents to come through the Elland Road ranks over the the past couple of years is Harry Kewell. Unfortunately for Wilkinson, top clubs demand instant success, and Wilkinson was sacked in the summer of 1996. It is David O'Leary who is now reaping the benefit of that early spadework, although Wilkinson is the first to pay tribute to the way the Irishman has brought Kewell and co into the first team.

Kewell control

Wilkinson signed Kewell as a 16-year-old from New South Wales Soccer Academy, in December 1995. The fee was just £2,400. When Kewell came over to Elland Road for trials, he actually played at left-back. Wilkinson and Gordon Strachan - the club captain at the time - saw in his technical ability and first-rate attitude the potential for him to make a big impression on the game. Now 21, Kewell is one of the best left-sided attacking players in the Premiership. With excellent control and terrific pace he can go past players either way - rather like his hero when he was growing up in Sydney, Paul Gascoigne.

Kewell's growing reputation

He is committed to playing for his native country, and was devastated when Australia missed out on a World Cup place at France '98. Kewell scored against Iran in both legs of the critical qualifier, but Australia went out on

away goals. Realistically, however, as far as top honours in the game are concerned, Kewell will have to look to club football. With Leeds in the coming season's Champions' League, Kewell will be stepping up to face the next big challenge. He will also inevitably be putting himself in the shop window, and there has already been speculation that he is being tracked by some of the top Italian clubs.

The future at Elland Road

Needless to say, O'Leary will be desperate to keep a player that he regards as having the potential to become one of the game's greats. O'Leary sees Manchester United as the team which sets the standard, as Wilkinson did before him. He recognises that having finished 4th and 3rd in the last two seasons, the only way to go on and break the stranglehold United have had on the Premiership is to keep Kewell and co at Elland Road.

PLAYER PROFILE

FULL NAME	Harold Kewell
DATE OF BIRTH	22 September 1978
BIRTHPLACE	Smithfield, Australia
HEIGHT	6'0"
WEIGHT	11st 10lbs
POSITION	Midfielder
TRANSFER	23 December 1995 from the Australian Academy of Sport

	Appearances	Goals
League '99/2000	36	10

CLUB HONOURS FA Youth Cup 1997

INTERNATIONAL HONOURS Australia

THIRTY-FIVE-YARDER

Kewell's goal tally last season, 10 goals from 36 games, is respectable. Among them were some spectacular strikes, such as the 35-yarder he got against Aston Villa at Elland Road.

HARRY KEWELL

If you were to separate out all the different footballing skills and pick the best exponents of those individual arts, then Georgi Kinkladze would have to be very near the top of the "Dribbling" category. His close control while travelling at pace is phenomenal. Defenders know there is no point waiting for him to lose the ball, so they are forced to commit themselves. They often find themselves lunging for a ball that isn't there any more; Kinkladze has already gone!

Breathtaking skills

Born in Tbilisi, Georgia, Kinkladze was a footballing prodigy. He was playing in the famous Dynamo side by the time he was 17, and for the national team by the age of 21. Financial problems forced the club to part with their star player. Dynamo let him go on loan to Germany, and it was while he was there that he came to the attention of Manchester City manager Alan Ball. After seeing a video of Kinkladze in action, the City boss paid £2m to bring him to Maine Road. He made his debut for City in August 1995, and his breathtaking skills soon made him an idol of the Maine Road fans.

Goal of the season

Unfortunately, Manchester City were a struggling side at the time. Kinkladze was the star turn, but there just weren't enough quality supporting acts. It seemed at times that Kinkladze played the opposition on his own. In fact, in one memorable match against Southampton, in March 1996, he did exactly that, dancing his way through the entire Saints defence to score one of the best goals of that season or any other.

Georgi's virtuoso displays

Kinkladze's virtuoso displays weren't quite enough, though, and City were relegated to Division One at the end of the 1995-96 season. A lot of top players have a habit of deserting sinking ships, but, to his credit, Kinkladze stayed on at Maine Road. Things went from bad to worse, however, and City went into free-fall. Opposing teams knew that if they could cut off the supply to or from Kinkladze, then the leaky City defence would do the rest. The team survived the 1996-97 season, but suffered the drop again a year later.

Kinkladze and Ajax

No one could accuse Kinkladze of just looking out for his own interests, but he did eventually leave Maine Road as City were relegated to Division Two. The £5m move to Ajax seemed perfect for him. He was joining a club whose name was synonymous with producing technically gifted players. At last he would be surrounded by players on the same wavelength as himself. It didn't quite work out like that, however. Kinkladze suffered a loss in form, something he felt was down to being played out of position. Then there was a change in manager, and Kinkladze found himself languishing in the reserves.

Georgi the Ram

That was how things stood when Jim Smith took a chance and brought him to Derby halfway through last season. It was initially a loan deal, but the Bald Eagle made it permanent by paying £3m for him in April of this year. His form was patchy at first, largely down to a lack of fitness. But even when he couldn't last 90 minutes, he still showed glimpses of his wonderful talent.

PLAYER PROFILE

FULL NAME	Georgiou Kinkladze
DATE OF BIRTH	6 November 1973
BIRTHPLACE	Tbilisi, Georgia
HEIGHT	5'8"
WEIGHT	12st 10lbs
POSITION	Midfielder
TRANSFER	19 April 2000 from Ajax
FEE	£3 million

	Appearances	Goals
League '99/2000	17	1

MAINE TRIBUTE FOR KINKLADZE Perhaps the greatest testimony to Kinkladze's ability comes from the Manchester City fans who once marvelled at his performances. When a player leaves a club, the adoration of the fans usually evaporates at the same time. But since Kinkladze's return to British football, some of the Maine Road faithful have made the journey to Derby to see him grace the football field once again. In these days of fierce rivalry between clubs, that is some tribute.

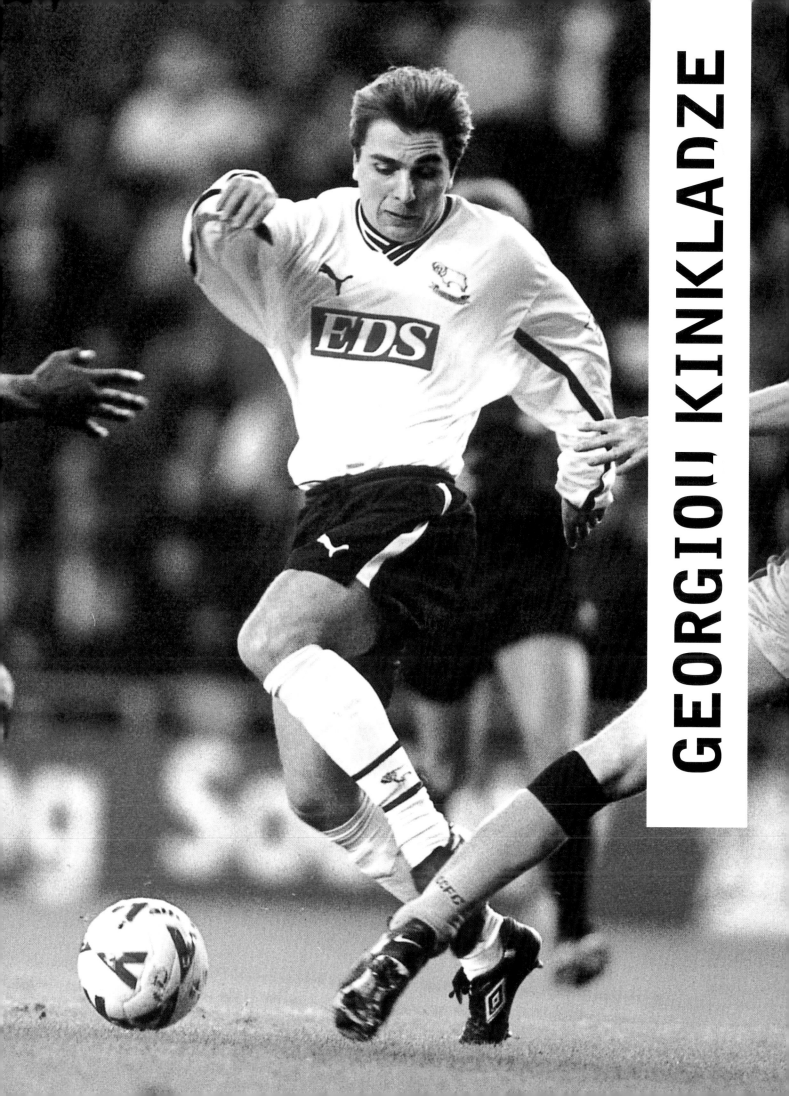

GEORGIOU KINKLADZE

When Paul Merson's name is mentioned, two images immediately spring to mind. One is the jubilant player dancing round the Wembley pitch after Arsenal's 1993 League Cup win over Sheffield Wednesday. Merson mimes to the crowd what the victory celebrations will consist of: downing large quantities of alcohol. The second image, just a year later, is the press conference in which Merson is reduced to tears as he goes public over his addiction to drugs and gambling, as well as alcohol.

Speed of thought

Merson was the golden boy at Arsenal. He spent ten years at Highbury, during which time he helped the club to win five major trophies. As a player, he is no slouch over the ground, but it it is his speed of thought which is more important. Either with a killer pass or surging run, his inventiveness playing behind the main strikers has made him the kind of player who can unlock defences.

Merson and England

In 1997, Merson looked to have got his career back on track by swapping London's glitzy lifestyle for a new challenge on Teesside, with Bryan Robson's Middlesbrough. Initially, everything went brilliantly. In Division One a rejuvenated Merson stood out head and shoulders above the rest. He was superb in the promotion-winning campaign of 1997-98, and it was no surprise when he won back his England place after an absence of four years. He celebrated his recall by scoring, in a win over Switzerland.

Class act

Merson's roller-coaster career then took another dip, however. He announced that he wanted away from the Riverside Stadium, citing as his reason the fact that there was a culture at the club that threatened to drag him back into his bad old ways. Bryan Robson denied the charge, but Merson was adamant and he joined Aston Villa in a £6.75m deal. It was an awful lot of money for a 30-year-old, but Merson settled into the Villa side well and showed again what a class act he is.

Off-field problems

During the 1998-99 season, his off-field problems resurfaced, and Villa were faced with the prospect of having a very expensive liability on their hands. Up to the Christmas period of last season he had played just four full games. Villa were playing badly and went into free-fall in the league. John Gregory was many pundits' favourite as the next managerial casualty.

Back to his best

The revival in Merson's form and the club's fortunes were almost an exact mirror image of each other. Back in the side and playing as well as ever, Merson was at the heart of Villa's outstanding second half of the season. The team went on a run which saw them lose just twice in the league and reach the FA Cup Final.

PLAYER PROFILE

FULL NAME	Paul Charles Merson
DATE OF BIRTH	20 March 1968
BIRTHPLACE	Harlesden, England
HEIGHT	6'0"
WEIGHT	13st 2lbs
POSITION	Forward
TRANSFER	10 Sept 1998 from Middlesbrough
FEE	£6.75 million

	Appearances	Goals
League '99/2000	32	5
England	21	

CLUB HONOURS Division One 89, 91; League Cup 93; FA Cup 93; Cup Winners Cup 94
INTERNATIONAL HONOURS England Youth; England Under-21; England B International; England

MERSON'S FUTURE The FA Cup Final itself was a disappointment. Merson didn't find his touch, and that was probably a major factor in Villa's lacklustre performance. That defeat ought not to take the shine off Merson's great form in recent months, though. Merson said after the Cup Final that he hopes to stay at Villa Park, but that there is a distinct possibility that he might be on the move again during the summer. If so, he has shown that he is still a top performer, even at 32, and there will surely be a queue of clubs ready and waiting to snap him up.

An expression that has entered footballing language over the last ten years is "Doing a Gascoigne". It is shorthand for cruciate knee ligament damage that is so severe it can end a career. Alternatively, as in Gazza's case, players may recover but find they have lost a yard of pace. Marc Overmars "did a Gascoigne" while playing for Ajax at the Olympic Stadium in Amsterdam. It was an innocent enough moment during a league match. He was pushed by an opponent near the touchline, but on this occasion it sent him crashing into one of the advertising hoardings that surround the pitch.

Battle for fitness

Overmars was 22 at the time, He was already an established international, and had a European Cup winner's medal to his name, Ajax having beaten AC Milan in the 1995 final. The injury put paid to any hope of his appearing at Euro '96. Overmars therefore missed the tournament which included England's comprehensive victory over the Dutch. He had the long, hard battle back to fitness to contend with.

Electric pace

As his nickname "Roadrunner" suggests, Overmar's game is all about pace. The skill and touch wouldn't desert him, but would he recapture that electric burst of speed that takes him past players? When he had recovered physically from the injury, the all-important sprint times were measured, and it was found that Roadrunner was indeed still capable of disappearing in a cloud of dust!

Quality finishing

Arsène Wenger took Overmars to Highbury in the summer of 1997. Like Bergkamp before him, he took a little while to adjust to the Premiership. But he then settled into to his role on Arsenal's left flank, where he was both an intelligent provider and a quality finisher.

Overmars at the double

An example of the latter came when the Gunners went to Old Trafford, on 14 March 1998. It was a tight game in which a classy combination of pace and cool finishing by Overmars was the difference between the two sides. He raced on to an Anelka flick, nodded the ball on with his first touch, then slotted it past the advancing Schmeichel to score the only goal of the match. It was a vital turning point of the season. Arsenal cut United's lead at the top of the table to just six points, with three games in hand. Wenger's team went on to win the Premiership, and Overmars made it a memorable first season by scoring the opening goal in a 2-0 win over Newcastle in the FA Cup Final.

World Cup '98

Overmars went straight into the World Cup off the back of this triumphant double, but things didn't go as well for him at France '98. He was in excellent form for the powerful Dutch side, when he sustained a hamstring injury. He played just 30 minutes of the quarter-final tie against Argentina, but that didn't prove too costly as his Arsenal team-mate Bergkamp conjured up a wonder strike late in the game. It was the disappointing semi-final exit against Brazil where Overmars was sorely missed. Holland coach Guus Hiddink believed that a fit Overmars might have made the difference that day.

PLAYER PROFILE

FULL NAME	Marc Overmars
DATE OF BIRTH	29 March 1973
BIRTHPLACE	Ernst, Holland
HEIGHT	5'8"
WEIGHT	11st 4lbs
POSITION	Midfielder
TRANSFER	10 July 1997 from Ajax
FEE	£7 million

	Appearances	Goals
League '99/2000	31	7
Holland	51	

CLUB HONOURS Premier League 98; FA Cup 98; Charity Shield 99
INTERNATIONAL HONOURS Holland
CHAMPIONS' LEAGUE More recently, Overmars was the pick of an out-of-sorts Arsenal which lost in last season's UEFA Cup Final against Galatasaray. Almost immediately, there was speculation that he may be on his way out of Highbury. But Arsenal have a new Champions' League challenge before them, a competition the club has under-performed in in recent years. Overmars is a gritty, determined character who has shown how he responds to challenges.

MARC OVERMARS

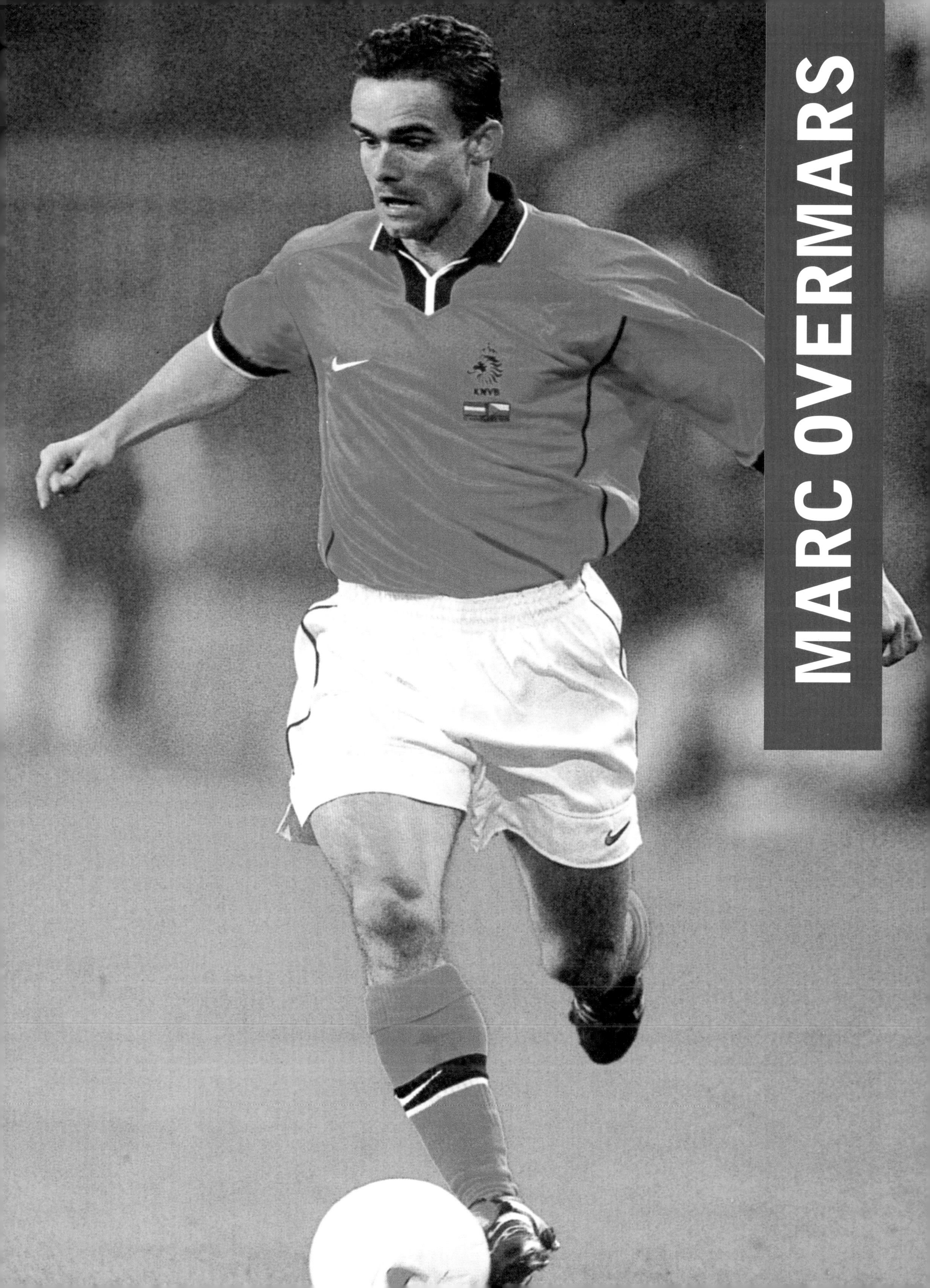

ichael Owen has been such a key member of both the Liverpool and England teams for so long that it is easy to forget that the Chester-born star is still only 20.

Owen exploded on to the Premiership scene as a 17-year-old, given his first-team chance by Gerard Houllier's predecessor at Anfield, Roy Evans. The maxim 'if you're good enough, you're old enough' might have been written with Owen in mind. He looked very young and innocent, but he knew how to put himself about and unsettle defenders.

Electrifying pace

In the modern era, talent alone is not enough. The game is played at such a high tempo that pace is vital, especially for a striker. And when it comes to pace, few can match Owen's electrifying turn of speed.

Scoring debut

He began terrorising defences and plundering goals right from the outset. He scored on his debut at Wimbledon on 6 May 1997, and went on to net 30 goals in the next season, a haul which earned him the 1997-98 PFA Young Player of the Year award.

England's youngest

The icing on the cake was still to come, though. For at the age of just 18 years and 59 days Owen was capped for England. He became the youngest player this century to play for the national team, beating the record of one of the famous Manchester United Busby Babes, Duncan Edwards. Owen was 124 days younger than Edwards when he made his impressive debut in a friendly against Chile. Less than four months later he also became the youngest player to score for England, when he found the net in a World Cup warm-up match against Morocco.

World Cup '98

But that was just to get the team and the country in the mood for biggest stage of all: France '98. The pundits clamoured for Owen's inclusion in the team, but Hoddle initially left him out. When England played against the seeded team of the group, Romania, the side went 1-0 down. Owen was thrown on as substitute and hit the equaliser. Although Chelsea's Dan Petrescu scored an injury-time winner for Romania, Owen had assured himself of a place in the starting line-up. It was Owen's blistering run and memorable strike in the match against Argentina, however, which made him one of the stars of the tournament.

Owen's injury setback

In the 1998-99 season he took up where he left off - banging in the goals for Liverpool: 18 in the Premiership, 23 in total. The first setback to Owen's career came when he sustained a hamstring injury while playing against Leeds in April '99. It sidelined him for longer than expected, and limited his first-team appearances last season to just 27.

PLAYER PROFILE

FULL NAME	Michael James Owen
DATE OF BIRTH	14 December 1979
BIRTHPLACE	Chester, England
HEIGHT	5'9"
WEIGHT	11st 2lbs
POSITION	Forward
TRANSFER	Signed as trainee

	Appearances	Goals
League '99/2000	27	11
England	19	6

AWARDS Carling Player of the Year 1997-98; BBC Sports Personality Of The Year 1998; Premiership Golden Boot 1997-98 and 1998-99 (both shared); World Cup FIFA Squad Of The Tournament, 1998.

CLUB HONOURS FA Youth Cup 1996

INTERNATIONAL HONOURS England Schoolboy; England Youth; England Under-21; England

OWEN'S FUTURE Kevin Keegan will be hoping for a fully fit Michael Owen when the serious business of World Cup 2002 gets under way. On the domestic front, Liverpool fans will be hoping Owen steers clear of injury in the coming season. With Robbie Fowler returning from a long-term lay-off, and Heskey and Camara also available, it will be interesting to see how Gerard Houllier rotates his strikers in 2000-2001.

MICHAEL OWEN

The media love nothing better than to give a rising star a label. A particular favourite is to compare an emerging talent to a famous player from the past. For a long time Ryan Giggs had to put up with being labelled "the new George Best". The difference with Marian Pahars is that the player he is compared to is hardly a has-been himself - for the Southampton striker has been dubbed "The Latvian Michael Owen". Naturally, Pahars was flattered by the comparison at first. But now that he has established himself as one of the most skilful and stylish attacking players in the country, Pahars finds any comparison to the Liverpool star rather tiresome.

Blinding goals

The Latvian international signed for Saints from Skonto Riga just before the transfer deadline in March 1999. He impressed then Saints boss Dave Jones in a trial match - by doing absolutely nothing for most of the game, then popping up to score three blinding goals!

Pahars at the Dell

Not surprisingly, Jones was keen to complete the transfer, but the club encountered work permit problems. The application for a permit was refused twice, Pahars not being considered good enough! The club persisted and the third appeal was successful: Southampton had their man.

Diving header

In the tense, end-of-season run-in, Pahars scored a vital equaliser in the home match against Blackburn, after coming on as substitute. Then in the final home game of the season, he scored both goals against Everton in a 2-0 win. The second, a terrific diving header, sent Saints fans wild as it sealed their Premiership survival for another year.

Constant threat

After a great start to last season, Pahars went through a barren spell in mid-season.

But when Glenn Hoddle took over at the club in February, it coincided with a return to favour and form for Pahars. The Latvian's goals helped Southampton to be clear of relegation danger long before the last match of the season. In fact, when Wimbledon came to the Dell on 14 May, it was the visitors who needed a result. Pahars was a constant threat to the Dons that day, and it was he who sealed their fate with a fantastic solo effort. The Saints were already 1-0 up when he ran the length of the field, beat two players and drove the ball past Neil Sullivan.

Following Shearer's path

Pahars's 13 goals out of Southampton's Premiership total of just 45 might not seem overly impressive. But 13 goals at a club which always seems to be in a relegation dogfight might well be worth considerably more in a better side which creates better chances. A certain young striker called Alan Shearer scored exactly 13 League goals for Southampton in 1991-92, his last season with the club before his big-money move to Blackburn. His strike record thereafter is, as they say, history.

PLAYER PROFILE

FULL NAME	Marian Pahars
DATE OF BIRTH	5 August 1976
BIRTHPLACE	Latvia
HEIGHT	5'9"
WEIGHT	10st 9lbs
POSITION	Forward
TRANSFER	25 March 1999 from Skonto Riga
FEE	£800,000

	Appearances	Goals
League '99/2000	34	13
Latvia	18	

INTERNATIONAL HONOURS Latvia

PAHARS'S HOT STREAK
Last season Pahars got off to a flying start, netting 7 times in the first 11 games. He was in the middle of this hot streak when Southampton went to Old Trafford in September. Pahars scored a gem of a goal, nutmegging Jaap Stam before slotting the ball home. It helped the Saints to a very creditable 3-3 draw.

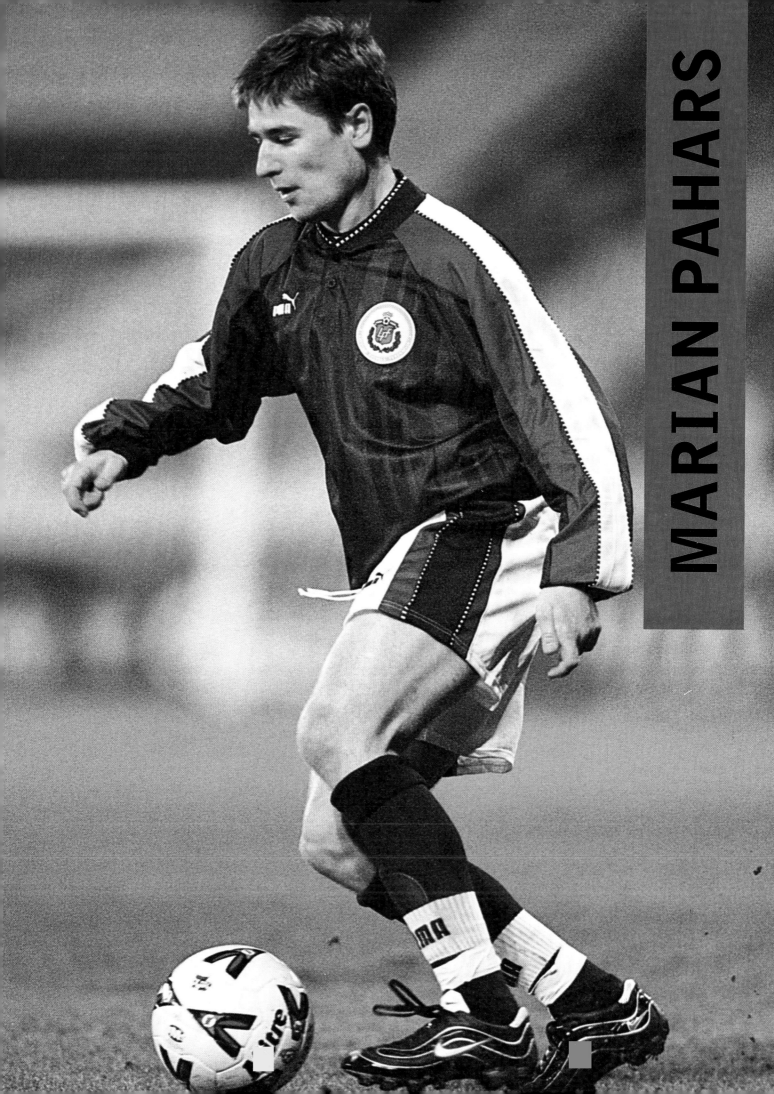

MARIAN PAHARS

For Emmanuel Petit, the 1998-99 season was something of an anti-climax - as indeed it was bound to be. For the previous season, his first at Highbury, had ended with Arsenal winning the double. Petit had then joined the French team for their World Cup triumph on home soil. He had played at the heart of the midfield and was widely acclaimed for his consistent performances. And, for good measure, he had stroked home his side's third goal in that famous 3-0 win over Brazil. The fact that it was against the country with the most illustrious World Cup pedigree rounded off a storybook year for Petit. Nor did his lucky streak stop there. For that same summer he casually dropped a coin into a Monte Carlo casino - and scooped a £17,000 jackpot!

Adjusting to English football

That 10-month period was some act to follow. Petit rejoined the Arsenal squad for the new season late, given extra time to recover from his summer's exertions. When he did return for the 1998-99 campaign, he struggled to find his best form, and this wasn't helped by a succession of run-ins with referees. The resulting suspensions apparently made Petit consider quitting Highbury, and not for the first time. He had been on the verge of leaving a year earlier, not long after his £3.5m move from Monaco. He had found it difficult adjusting to the mental and physical pressures of playing in the Premiership.

Classy playmaker

Arsène Wenger managed to talk the player round during both crises. He knew Petit well, having had him at Monaco as a young left-back. Wenger didn't want to lose this vital cog in the Arsenal machine. An elegant player with the sweetest of left feet, Petit is one of the driving forces in midfield. Along with Patrick Vieira, he gives excellent protection to the defence, snuffing out opposition attacks before they develop. When Arsenal are in possession, he likes to get forward and is a classy playmaker. Many sides have a holding player and a creative player in midfield; Petit is one of those rare talents who can do both jobs. He is terrific

from box to box, and has, as the coaches say, "a good engine", vital for covering so much ground.

Champions' League

Last season it was a case of nearly but not quite, as Arsenal had to be content with the runners-up spot in both the Premiership and the UEFA Cup. As the season drew to a close, it looked like Wenger might again have his work cut out in keeping the influential midfielder at Highbury for another year.

Petit's future

Approaching 30, and having achieved so much in his three seasons at Arsenal, some believe it will not be long before he returns to the continent. His frustration with the disciplinary problems that have dogged him is well known. The one thing that might persuade him to stay is the prospect of another crack at the Champions' League, a competition in which Arsenal have underachieved in recent years.

PLAYER PROFILE

FULL NAME	Emmanuel Petit
DATE OF BIRTH	22 September 1970
BIRTHPLACE	Dieppe, France
HEIGHT	6'1"
WEIGHT	12st 7lbs
POSITION	Midfielder
TRANSFER	25 June 1997 from AS Monaco
FEE	£3.5 million

	Appearances	Goals
League '99/2000	26	3
France	29	

CLUB HONOURS Premier League 1998; FA Cup 1998; Charity Shield 1998

INTERNATIONAL HONOURS France

BACK TO HIS BEST
Although Petit's second season at Highbury produced no silverware, at least he had survived the rocky patch which had nearly led to him turning his back on the Premiership. He was more settled and playing well again.

EMMANUEL PETIT

Although Roy Keane was an overwhelmingly popular choice as Player of the Year last season, when Keane was asked who he himself would vote for he immediately nominated Kevin Phillips. Sunderland's ace striker was the Premiership's hotshot, hitting the magical 30-goal mark for the 1999-2000 season. This was a remarkable achievement, considering it was his first taste of top-flight football. 'Superkev' - as he is called by the Wearside club's fans - had struck 25 goals in the promotion-winning campaign of 1998-99, despite missing three months of the season through injury. And when he arrived on the Premiership stage he just kept banging them in.

Phillips's rise to the top

Phillips must still occasionally pinch himself over his fairytale rise to the top. He began his career at Southampton, where he cleaned Alan Shearer's boots, but he was not considered good enough for the professional ranks by Saints manager Chris Nicholl. He ended up working at Dixon's and turning out for Baldock Town. He could easily have sunk without trace in non-League football, but even then he was determined to show Nicholl that he had made a mistake in letting him go.

Emergency striker

Phillips played both in defence and midfield for Baldock, but it was when he was pressed into service as an emergency striker during an injury crisis that he got his big break. For it was while playing up front that he caught the eye of Watford boss Graham Taylor, who took him to Vicarage Road for just £10,000 in December 1994. Phillips grabbed his second chance of making it in League football with both hands. Another huge setback occurred then, however, this time in the shape of a career-threatening injury. It

kept him out of action for a year, but he showed his determination by battling back to full fitness.

The buy of the decade

Peter Reid paid £600,000 for Phillips in July 1997, which must go down as one of the shrewdest deals ever done by the Wearside club - or any other club, for that matter. Niall Quinn had already been at the club a year and in the three years that the pair have played together they have earned a reputation as a formidable strike pairing, capable of unsettling any defence.

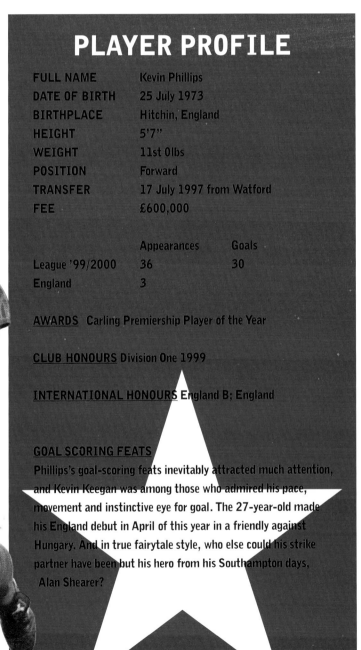

PLAYER PROFILE

FULL NAME	Kevin Phillips
DATE OF BIRTH	25 July 1973
BIRTHPLACE	Hitchin, England
HEIGHT	5'7"
WEIGHT	11st 0lbs
POSITION	Forward
TRANSFER	17 July 1997 from Watford
FEE	£600,000

	Appearances	Goals
League '99/2000	36	30
England	3	

AWARDS Carling Premiership Player of the Year

CLUB HONOURS Division One 1999

INTERNATIONAL HONOURS England B; England

GOAL SCORING FEATS
Phillips's goal-scoring feats inevitably attracted much attention, and Kevin Keegan was among those who admired his pace, movement and instinctive eye for goal. The 27-year-old made his England debut in April of this year in a friendly against Hungary. And in true fairytale style, who else could his strike partner have been but his hero from his Southampton days, Alan Shearer?

KEVIN PHILLIPS

anagers love to have strikers in their side who can put away 20 goals in a season. But to be successful in the modern game goals have to come from other areas of the pitch. The midfielder who times his forward run and arrives late in the box is a great asset to any team. Such players are often the most difficult for defences to pick up. But getting forward is one thing; banging in the chances is another. Gus Poyet does both, to devastating effect. He is undoubtedly one of the best exponents of attacking midfield play in the country.

Classy Poyet

Poyet signed for Chelsea just short of his 30th birthday, in the summer of 1997. Much has been said about the age and quality of some of the overseas players who have come to the Premiership, but Poyet must be regarded as a classy exception to such criticism. The Uruguayan international's record, impressive though it is, would have been even better had his time at Stamford Bridge not been blighted by injury. He sustained cruciate knee ligament damage early in his first season with the club, and didn't return until April. He still managed 5 goals from 16 starts that year, but Chelsea sorely missed him.

Phenomenal scoring rate

He started the following season on fire, scoring 10 goals in the games up to Christmas. And in the middle of this great scoring run, he also hit the goal that brought the Blues their fourth piece of silverware in less than 18 months. It was a right-footed drive from the edge of the box that beat Real Madrid and won Chelsea the European Super Cup. Poyet's form in the early part of that 1998-99 season played a large part in taking Chelsea to the top of the league for the first time in nine years. Not only was his scoring rate phenomenal, but his all-round midfield play was top-notch. His tackling, passing and quality on the ball, combined with a tremendous work-rate, made him the pick of the Premiership midfielders during that spell.

Poyet's hot streak

Chelsea went 18 matches unbeaten during Poyet's hot streak. He was then struck down by injury again, in a match against Southampton at the Dell. Poyet had already scored, when he took a knock to the same knee that kept him out for much of the previous season. The injury sidelined him for almost four months, during which time Chelsea were not the same force.

Match-winner

He returned in time for the Cup Winners' Cup semi-final defeat against Real Mallorca in April 1999. But he was back in scoring form in the vital Premiership match against Leeds, when both clubs were vying for a Champions' League spot. Poyet hit the match-winner, one of his trademark towering headers, and Chelsea edged out their Yorkshire rivals for a place in the elite competition.

PLAYER PROFILE

FULL NAME	Gustavo Augusto Poyet
DATE OF BIRTH	15 November 1967
BIRTHPLACE	Montevideo, Uruguay
HEIGHT	6'2"
WEIGHT	13st 0lbs
POSITION	Midfielder
TRANSFER	15 July 1997 from Real Zaragoza
FEE	Free

	Appearances	Goals
League '99/2000	33	10
Uruguay	23	

CLUB HONOURS Cup Winners' Cup 1998; European Super Cup 1998

INTERNATIONAL HONOURS Uruguay

FA CUP TRIUMPH Last season, Poyet was again out of the blocks quickly, with two goals against newly-promoted Sunderland, one of them a glorious volley. It set him on the road to another 10-goal haul for the season. It ended with FA Cup triumph, but Poyet is desperate to win the Premiership with Chelsea. If the club is to challenge for the title, then an in-form Poyet will be crucial. For the last three years have shown that when Poyet plays well, so does the team as a whole.

GUSTAVO POYET

Some players choose to bow out of football at the top, some choose to drop down a division or two when it is felt that they are past their prime. Not many drop out of the top flight then storm back years later, the wrong side of 30, to make an impact all over again. At 33, Niall Quinn is undoubtedly in the autumn of a long and illustrious career, but he has enjoyed a marvellous return to the Premiership with Peter Reid's exciting Sunderland team.

Perfect partner

Although it is the free-scoring Kevin Phillips who grabs most of the headlines, he is the first to pay tribute to Quinn's contribution. At 6ft 4in Quinn is a handful for any defence in the air, but is also capable of deft touches on the deck, and Phillips has his partner to thank for many assists.

Gunner Quinn

Quinn began his career at Arsenal, making his League debut as a teenager in 1985. He scored 14 goals in 67 League appearances for the Gunners, and helped them to League Cup success in 1987 before moving to Manchester City in 1990 for £800,000. Peter Reid was a City player at the time, but Quinn got his first taste of calling Reid 'Boss' when he was appointed manager at Maine Road.

Record deal

Six years later, Quinn was nearly 30 and languishing in a struggling Manchester City side when Reid, now at Sunderland, brought his former player to join him. The £1.3m deal was a record for the Wearside club.

Quinn's honour

Quinn had the honour of scoring the first ever goal at Sunderland's Stadium of Light - ironically in a 3-1 win over his former club Manchester City. Sunderland had just won promotion to the Premiership, but it was not a happy experience, either for Quinn or the club. The genial Irishman missed most of the season through injury and the team made an instant return back to Division One.

Player of the Year

Quinn scored twice in a dramatic play-off against Charlton at the end of the 1997-98 season, but ended on the losing side. The following year they made no mistake. 1998-99 was a champagne season for the club as they became Division One champions at a canter. Quinn scored 21 goals during the season and was made Sunderland's Player of the Year.

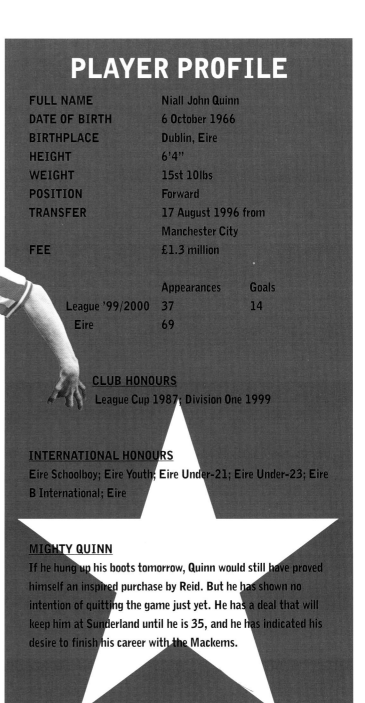

PLAYER PROFILE

FULL NAME	Niall John Quinn
DATE OF BIRTH	6 October 1966
BIRTHPLACE	Dublin, Eire
HEIGHT	6'4"
WEIGHT	15st 10lbs
POSITION	Forward
TRANSFER	17 August 1996 from Manchester City
FEE	£1.3 million

	Appearances	Goals
League '99/2000	37	14
Eire	69	

CLUB HONOURS
League Cup 1987; Division One 1999

INTERNATIONAL HONOURS
Eire Schoolboy; Eire Youth; Eire Under-21; Eire Under-23; Eire B International; Eire

MIGHTY QUINN
If he hung up his boots tomorrow, Quinn would still have proved himself an inspired purchase by Reid. But he has shown no intention of quitting the game just yet. He has a deal that will keep him at Sunderland until he is 35, and he has indicated his desire to finish his career with the Mackems.

NAILL QUINN

Not since the days of Klinsmann, Sheringham and Barmby have Tottenham played the kind of scintillating, attacking football that White Hart Lane crowds demand. Spurs fans will be hoping that the arrival of Sergei Rebrov will bring the kind of style and clinical finishing that has been missing from the team in recent years. Rebrov might not be a household name yet, but his pedigree is impressive and he has the kind of quality that could make him a star in the Premiership.

London rivals

Several top clubs had been tracking the Ukrainian, including Rangers and Arsenal. The Gunners' Oleg Luzhny knows Rebrov well, having played with him for eight years at Dynamo Kiev. He remembers seeing Rebrov play as a 19-year-old, and recognised immediately what a special talent he was. Luzhny would have preferred Rebrov to come to Highbury; instead, the coming season's north London derby games will have the added spice of Ukrainian rivalry.

Champions' League

As Dynamo Kiev invariably sweep the board in domestic competition, it is in the Champions' League that the team's quality is tested. The side looked like genuine contenders to go all the way in 1997-98, with Rebrov and strike partner Andrei Shevchenko firing most of the bullets. In their run to the quarter-final they beat Barcelona 3-0 at home, and 4-0 in the return match at the Nou Camp. Although they eventually came unstuck against Juventus, the quality of the team - and in particular the strike pairing of Rebrov and Shevchenko - caught the eye.

Crucial goal

Arsenal's interest in Rebrov may have stemmed from the close encounter they had with him in the 1998-99 Champions' League campaign. The Gunners found themselves in the same group as Dynamo Kiev, and when the two sides met at Wembley, Shevchenko was outstanding, while Rebrov hit the goal which earned Kiev a 1-1 draw.

Spurs' record signing

The £11m Spurs have paid to bring Rebrov to White Hart Lane in a 5-year deal makes him easily the most expensive player to join the club. Ironically, the player who used to hold that dubious honour was Les Ferdinand, the £6m man from Newcastle who was also bought to add firepower to the Spurs team.

Spurs' overseas stars

Spurs have had mixed fortunes with the overseas stars they have brought in over the years. Ardiles made an incredible impact, as did Klinsmann in his first stint with the club; by contrast, the Romanian pair Popescu and Dumitrescu never lived up to their potential. With Ferdinand dogged by injury, Iversen not yet the finished article and Armstrong erratic in front of goal, Spurs are desperate for a player who converts a high percentage of chances into goals. Sergei Rebrov may just be the player they are looking for.

PLAYER PROFILE

FULL NAME	Sergei Rebrov
DATE OF BIRTH	3 March 1974
BIRTHPLACE	Ukraine
HEIGHT	5'7"
WEIGHT	9st 8lbs
POSITION	Forward
TRANSFER	16 May 2000 from Dynamo Kiev
FEE	£11 million

	Appearances	Goals
C. League '99/2000	12	8
Ukraine	28	9

<u>AWARDS</u> Ukrainian Best Footballer 96, 98

<u>CLUB HONOURS</u> Ukrainian Champion 93, 94, 95, 96, 97, 98, 99; Ukrainian Cup-winner 93, 96, 98, 99

<u>INTERNATIONAL HONOURS</u> Ukraine Under-21; Ukraine

<u>EUROPE'S TOP STRIKER</u> The ace partnership was broken up when Shevchenko departed in a big-money move. It was just a matter of time befor Rebrov followed suit, but he did hang on for one more crack at the Champions' League with Dynamo Kiev last season. And he put himself in the shop window in the most emphatic style possible. His eight goals against the likes of Bayern Munich, Lazio and eventual winners Real Madrid made him the top scorer in the competition.

SERGEI REBROV

amilton Ricard -'Ham the Man'- has undoubtedly proved himself to be one of Middlesbrough's best assets as the club has sought to establish itself as a Premiership force over the past couple of years. He arrived at the Riverside at the back end of Boro's promotion-winning campaign of 1997-98. Bryan Robson paid Deportivo Cali £2m for the 24-year-old, who had scored 77 goals in 160 games for the Colombian side.

Debut strike

He made his debut against Norwich City in March 1998, and got on the scoresheet for the first time in a match against Bury the following month. Generally, though, the Colombian international made a lacklustre start to his career on Teesside, and didn't immediately endear himself to the Boro fans. Both they and Robson were looking for better things; and he responded in blistering style when the team made the step up to the Premiership.

Hotshot Ricard

While most players find the gulf between Division One and the Premiership difficult to bridge, Ricard's class began to shine through when he faced top-flight opposition. He was the Premiership's hotshot in the early part of the 1998-99 campaign, and ended the season with 15 goals. That represented almost one third of Boro's total of 48. His goals went a long way to helping Boro secure a respectable 9th place in their return to the top level. Ricard's value to the side was underlined by the fact that his strike partner, Brian Deane, was the next highest scorer with just six goals.

Reliable goalscorer

The importance of having a reliable goalscorer such as Ricard at Premiership level was something that the two other promoted sides soon found out. Nottingham Forest and Charlton had both outscored the Teesside club in Division One, but found goals hard to come by in the Premiership. They hit just 35 and 41 goals respectively, and were relegated after one season.

Non-stop Ricard

The Colombian played the full 90 minutes in just 16 of Boro's Premiership matches last term, but he played some part in all but four of them. Having been involved in France '98 and Copa America in the summer of 1999 meant that Ricard had played virtually non-stop football for three years. He has been having an enforced break from the game this summer, however, recovering from a hernia problem. He missed the final game of last season, Boro's 2-0 win at Everton, and was due to have an operation almost immediately on the hernia condition that had been troubling him for some time.

The new campaign

Bryan Robson is confident that 26-year-old Ricard will be back in time for the new campaign, refreshed and ready to make it three years in a row as Boro's Number One hitman.

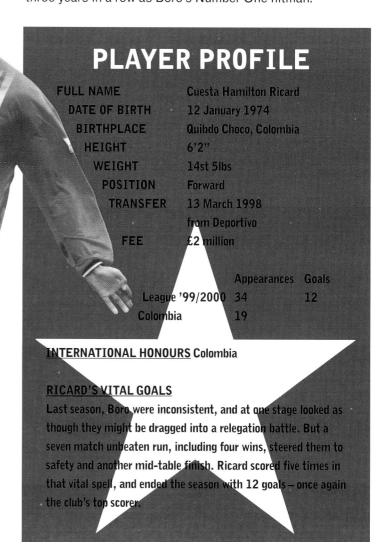

PLAYER PROFILE

FULL NAME	Cuesta Hamilton Ricard
DATE OF BIRTH	12 January 1974
BIRTHPLACE	Quibdo Choco, Colombia
HEIGHT	6'2"
WEIGHT	14st 5lbs
POSITION	Forward
TRANSFER	13 March 1998 from Deportivo
FEE	£2 million

	Appearances	Goals
League '99/2000	34	12
Colombia	19	

INTERNATIONAL HONOURS Colombia

RICARD'S VITAL GOALS
Last season, Boro were inconsistent, and at one stage looked as though they might be dragged into a relegation battle. But a seven match unbeaten run, including four wins, steered them to safety and another mid-table finish. Ricard scored five times in that vital spell, and ended the season with 12 goals – once again the club's top scorer.

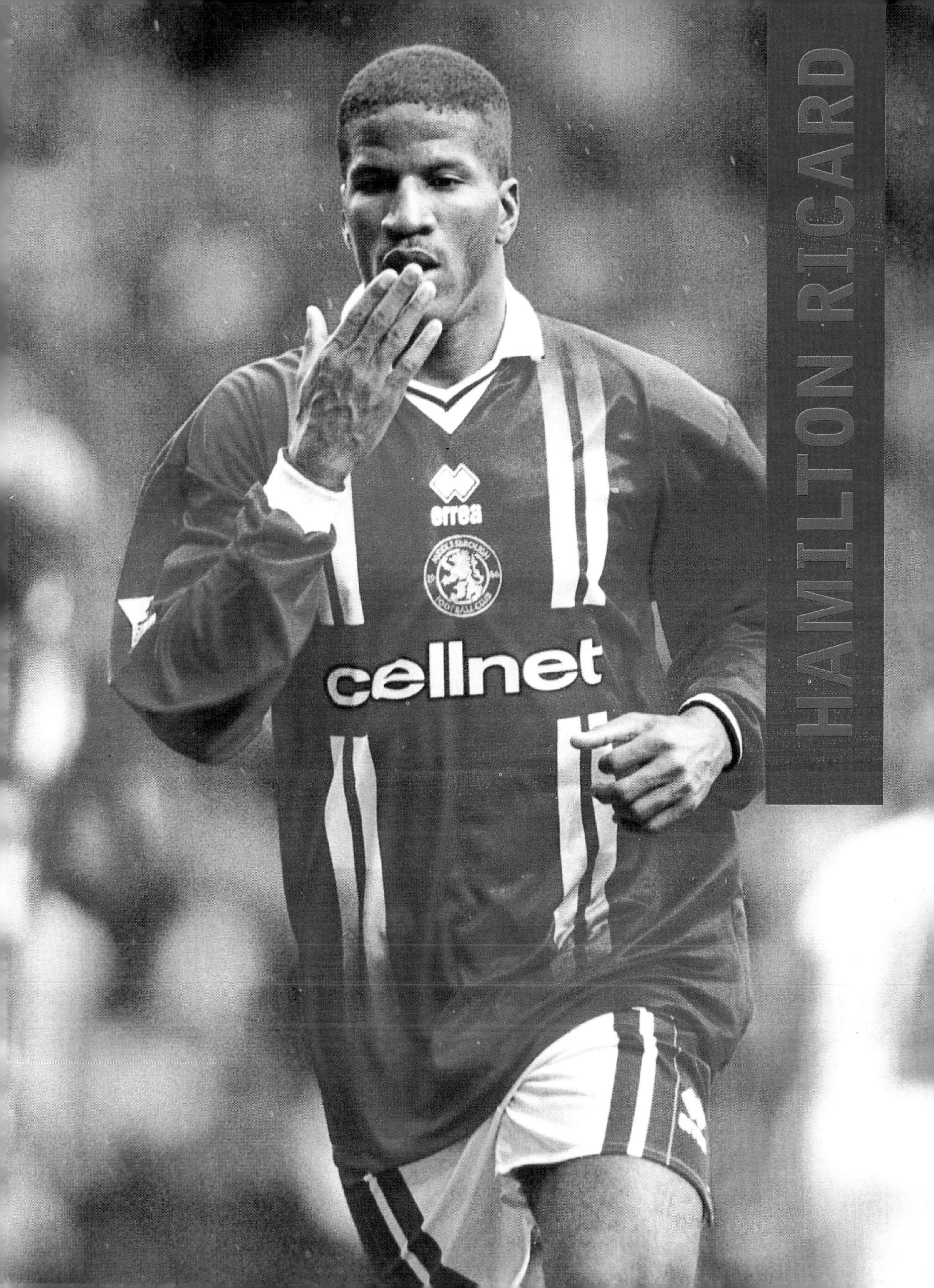
HAMILTON RICARD
errea
cellnet

Even after so many years at the top, at both club and international level, Alan Shearer still manages to divide opinion. No great pace, can't dribble, hasn't got any striker's tricks to speak of, say the detractors. Terrific movement, excellent in the air, thunderous shot, Shearer fans retort. As the country's premier striker for the best part of a decade, the final decision ought to rest with the stats: the first player in the Premiership to reach 100 goals; 30-plus goals in three successive seasons; the Premiership's top scorer in 1995, 1996 and 1997; top scorer at Euro '96, and an international haul close to a goal every two games. With a record like that, Shearer has to go down as one of the all-time greats.

Record deals

He has moved clubs for a record fee not once, but twice. Kenny Dalglish paid £3.6m to take the 21-year-old Shearer from Southampton to Blackburn in 1992. He was a veritable goal machine in his four years at Ewood Park, spearheading the club's rise to the top. Shearer was a major factor in Rovers' Premiership win in 1994-95, one of only two occasions that the title has left Old Trafford in the eight years it has been in existence.

15-million-pound man

Shearer's move to Newcastle for £15m in 1996 was a world record fee, and marked a return to his spiritual home. Once again, he ignored the price tag and got on with the business of scoring goals, leaving others to argue about whether he was worth that kind of money.

Shearer on Tyneside

Shearer's arrival at St James' Park was meant to be the vital piece in the jigsaw that would bring silverware to the club. But the past four years has been a period of turmoil and disruption on Tyneside, both for Shearer and the club as a whole. For the player, there was almost a year-long lay-off with an ankle injury. When he returned, the arguments over his effectiveness resumed even more fiercely. "Not the player he was" was a frequently heard comment. Yet, at 29, Shearer continues to let his goals do the talking for him. Last season he banged in another 23 goals in the Premiership, second only to Kevin Phillips. The Sunderland man has had a purple patch in scoring 30, but the record books show that Shearer does the business year in and year out.

Shearer's future

As far as Newcastle are concerned, Shearer will want Duncan Ferguson and himself to enjoy an injury-free run to build up their partnership. When they have played together, which hasn't been that often, they have shown signs of being a formidable pairing. Shearer has said he wants to concentrate his efforts for the Magpies for the remainder of his contract - effectively, the rest of his career. The critics will continue to snipe, but it is a racing certainty that the famous raised-arm salute will be seen many more times before he hangs up his boots.

PLAYER PROFILE

FULL NAME	Alan Shearer
DATE OF BIRTH	13 August 1970
BIRTHPLACE	Newcastle, England
HEIGHT	6'0"
WEIGHT	12st 6lbs
POSITION	Forward
TRANSFER	30 July 1996 from Blackburn Rovers
FEE	£15 million

	Appearances	Goals
League '99/00	37	23
England	57	28

AWARDS FA Premier League Hall of Fame 1995

CLUB HONOURS Premier League 1995

INTERNATIONAL HONOURS England Youth; England Under-21; England B International; England

SHEARER AND ENGLAND Shearer has announced that Euro 2000 will be his international swan-song. For years, successive England coaches have wrestled over who to play with Shearer. Michael Owen is the current favoured choice, though some feel they are not a natural pairing. Ironically, despite his record, it may be that Shearer's departure from the international scene will be a boon, allowing Keegan to experiment with other partnerships.

ALAN SHEARER

When a player is hailed as the pick of the crop of young talent at a club, it can mean very little. But when that club is Leeds United, where David O'Leary has a host of brilliant youngsters that he affectionately calls his 'babies', then the player in question must be very special.

Schoolboy star

Alan Smith is still only 19 and has had little more than a season playing in the Premiership. But the way he has adjusted to playing in the top flight has been very impressive. Others may have made their debuts earlier, but few have looked as classy or assured as this home-grown star that the Elland Road club has nurtured since the age of 10.

Smith's sensational debut

Smith made his first senior appearance in a game against Liverpool at Anfield in November 1998. He had only just celebrated his 18th birthday when he came on as substitute with Leeds 1-0 down, and promptly scored with his first touch after just two minutes on the pitch. Leeds went on to win the match 3-1.

Dream start

In his home debut the following week Smith scored again, helping his club to a 4-1 win over Charlton. This fabulous start to his career ensured him a regular first-team place and he also quickly became a big favourite with the Elland Road fans.

Eye for goal

He is sharp, stylish and cool under pressure, but also provides the kind of strong physical presence that lets defenders know they've been in a game. He has a true striker's eye for goal and is predatory in and around the box, but he plays with his head up and knows when the pass is the better option. When he does score, there is no delirious celebration; rather, he gives a simple raised-arm salute that has a tinge of confidence and arrogance about it. In fact, his style and demeanour have been compared to another gifted striker from the all-conquering Leeds side of the 1970s - Allan Clarke.

Champions' League

The point gained at West Ham in the final game of last season ensured Leeds would be in in the Champions' League for the first time. Smith, who was out through injuries for the start of the last campaign, is looking forward to the European challenge. With his coolness in the penalty box, his ability to score with both feet and with a maturity beyond his years, he will be a major asset as Leeds try to progress through the early rounds.

PLAYER PROFILE

FULL NAME	Alan Smith
DATE OF BIRTH	28 October 1980
BIRTHPLACE	Rothwell, England
HEIGHT	5'9"
WEIGHT	11st 10lbs
POSITION	Forward
TRANSFER	Signed as trainee

	Appearances	Goals
League '99/2000	24	4

INTERNATIONAL HONOURS
England Youth, England Under-21

FUTURE INTERNATIONAL
Smith has already represented England at Under-16, Under-18 and Under-21 level. Surprisingly few players have progressed through the ranks all the way to senior level, Terry Venables being one notable member of this exclusive club. Few would back against Alan Smith joining this select group and going on to make a big name for himself on the international stage.

ALAN SMITH

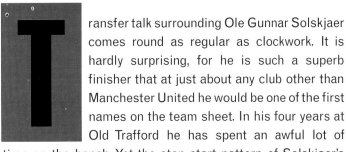

Transfer talk surrounding Ole Gunnar Solskjaer comes round as regular as clockwork. It is hardly surprising, for he is such a superb finisher that at just about any club other than Manchester United he would be one of the first names on the team sheet. In his four years at Old Trafford he has spent an awful lot of time on the bench. Yet the stop-start pattern of Solskjaer's career doesn't seem to affect him. When he does get his chance, he has the happy knack of being able to find the groove immediately.

Baby-faced Assassin

A look at Solskjaer's contribution in last season's Premiership campaign shows his immense worth. He featured in 28 of United's League matches and scored 12 goals. Not earth-shattering, but very respectable. The key word, though, is "featured". Solskjaer played the full 90 minutes in just 7 of those matches; in the other 21 games he made his more commonplace cameo appearances. If you add up the total amount of time that he actually spent on the pitch, it is the equivalent of less than 16 full games. 12 goals in 16 games: now that is special. With that kind of return and those youthful looks, it is no wonder he has earned himself the nickname "The Babyfaced Assassin" - something he dislikes, apparently.

Part-time in Norway

After playing part-time football in one of Norway's lower leagues, Solskjaer moved to Molde, one of the country's top sides, in 1995. It was while he was there that his goalscoring talent began to attract interest. He was dubbed "Norway's Alan Shearer", won the country's Player of the Year award for 1995-96 and was selected for the national team.

Ole at Old Trafford

In the summer of 1996, Alex Ferguson paid £1.5m to bring him to Old Trafford. He was an instant success, ending that first season as United's top scorer with 19 goals. His performances helped the club to win the Premiership title and reach the semi-final of the European Champions' League. When Dwight Yorke arrived, at the start of the 1998-99 season, rumours circulated that Solskjaer might be on his way out of Old Trafford. But the player confirmed that he wanted to stay at Old Trafford and fight for his place. And a long fight it would have to be, for Yorke and Cole were on fire.

Fairytale final

He found himself back on the bench for the Champions' League final against Bayern Munich in Barcelona, a match that will go down in football folklore, real Roy of the Rovers stuff. With time almost up and the team trailing 1-0, both Solskjaer and Teddy Sheringham had been thrown into the action. George Best had apparently already given it up as a lost cause and was making for the exit, when Sheringham swept the ball into the net. Deep into injury time, with extra time looming, Sheringham flicked on a Beckham corner and Solskjaer showed lightning reactions to put the ball into the roof of the net.

PLAYER PROFILE

FULL NAME	Ole Gunnar Solskjaer
DATE OF BIRTH	26 February 1973
BIRTHPLACE	Kristiansund, Norway
HEIGHT	5'10"
WEIGHT	11st 10lbs
POSITION	Forward
TRANSFER	29 July 1996 from Molde
FEE	£1.5 million

	Appearances	Goals
League '99/2000	28	12
Norway	22	

CLUB HONOURS Premier League 1997, 1999, 2000; FA Cup 1999; European Cup 1999

INTERNATIONAL HONOURS Norway

CLINICAL POACHER In that glorious treble-winning campaign, Solskjaer proved his value to the squad time and time again. In the 4th Round FA Cup tie against Liverpool he came on to hit a late winner, a clinical poacher's strike. It set United on the road to Wembley, where he had one of his rare starts for the team in the victory over Newcastle. As long as Solskjaer remains happy with his limited opportunities at United, United will surely be more than happy to keep him.

OLE GUNNAR SOLSKJAER

Match of the Day pundit Alan Hansen knows a thing or two about assessing players, summing up their strengths and weaknesses. But one player who has continually left him scratching his head is the eccentrically-talented Paulo Wanchope. The ex-Liverpool man has never quite been able to make up his mind whether Wanchope is a class act or class clown.

Paulo the enigma

Hansen's confusion has probably been shared by a lot of people. For it is easy to pick out pieces of terrific skill: the pacy Wanchope twisting and turning, those long gangling legs always managing to nick the ball away from defenders. But it is also easy to find examples of schoolboy errors. Such is the enigma called Paulo Wanchope.

Brilliant solo goal

The leggy Costa Rican made his first attempt to break into British football with a trial at QPR, but was unsuccessful. Derby's Jim Smith then took a look at him, and promptly signed him for £600,000.

Old Trafford debut

Debuts for a striker don't come much tougher than away at Old Trafford, and that is exactly what Wanchope faced in March 1997. He made an instant name for himself by scoring a brilliant solo goal, picking the ball up in a deep position and running at the heart of one of the meanest defences there is before slotting the ball home. It was a goal that encapsulated all that is best about his game.

Derby's top scorer

In his first full season for Derby, 1997-98, he was top scorer with 17 goals. He followed it up with 10 the season after. Harry Redknapp had seen enough to take him to Upton Park in the summer of 1999. He may have had plenty of raw edges, but he was still only 23. The fee of 3.5m, together with the £1.7m Redknapp had paid for Paolo Di Canio just a few months earlier, meant that the West Ham boss had acquired a fascinating strike duo for little more than £5m. It also left him with change to spare from the £7.5m that he had got from the sale of John Hartson to Wimbledon.

Amazing trickery

West Ham fans took the brilliant Di Canio to their hearts from the word go. Wanchope's erratic displays have meant that opinion remains divided on him. Redknapp has kept faith with the player, though. He speaks animatedly about the amazing things Wanchope can do with the ball in training, and will look to bring greater consistency to his game. Wanchope missed very few games last season and notched 12 goals. Not top-drawer finishing and nowhere near Di Canio's strike rate, but Wanchope is eight years the Italian's junior.

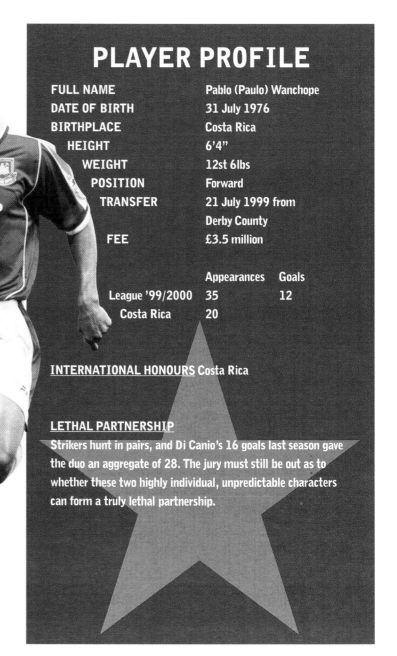

PLAYER PROFILE

FULL NAME	Pablo (Paulo) Wanchope
DATE OF BIRTH	31 July 1976
BIRTHPLACE	Costa Rica
HEIGHT	6'4"
WEIGHT	12st 6lbs
POSITION	Forward
TRANSFER	21 July 1999 from Derby County
FEE	£3.5 million

	Appearances	Goals
League '99/2000	35	12
Costa Rica	20	

INTERNATIONAL HONOURS Costa Rica

LETHAL PARTNERSHIP
Strikers hunt in pairs, and Di Canio's 16 goals last season gave the duo an aggregate of 28. The jury must still be out as to whether these two highly individual, unpredictable characters can form a truly lethal partnership.

PAULO WANCHOPE

The disarming smile which seems to be a permanent fixture on the face of Dwight Yorke should come with a warning - at least as far as opposition defences are concerned. For Yorke's happy-go-lucky demeanour belies his deadly intent when he is within striking distance of goal. He has the poaching instinct that all top strikers have - to be in the right place at the right time for bread-and-butter tap-ins- but he also has a flair for the spectacular.

Twelve-million-pound man

The record £12m price tag which took him from Aston Villa to Manchester United didn't weigh down the laid-back 26-year-old from Trinidad and Tobago; nor did the fact that he was taking his place at the Theatre of Dreams just after Eric Cantona had made his final exit from that illustrious stage. In fact, Yorke adopted Cantona's celebrated upturned collar - a stylish look to match his stylish play. He says he would love to emulate the kind of success that the Frenchman enjoyed at Old Trafford.

Electrifying partnership

Not all United fans were convinced by Yorke's arrival at the club in the summer of 1998. He had been a big fish at Aston Villa, but some thought he lacked the pedigree necessary for United's European campaigns, and that Ferguson ought to have gone for a proven, top-class striker from the continent. But Yorke immediately formed an electrifying partnership with Andy Cole, the goals started flying in and the doubters were quickly won over.

Treble-winning season

Even Alex Ferguson himself admitted that he was surprised at how quickly the two players found the groove, but it certainly gave him the spearhead for a brilliant treble-winning season. Yorke contributed 29 goals, and his consistent level of performance earned him the Carling Player of the Year award.

Fresh challenge

Yorke had stated that after nine happy years at Aston Villa, he had gone as far as he could with the club and needed a fresh challenge. He had set his sights on chasing top honours with the top club, and within a matter of months he had done just that. John Gregory's version of events was slightly different. He felt that Yorke's heart wasn't at Villa Park towards the end of his time there. 'All the jerseys hang together, but his wasn't on the same washing line,' as Gregory put it.

PLAYER PROFILE

FULL NAME	Dwight Yorke
DATE OF BIRTH	3 November 1971
BIRTHPLACE	Canaan, Tobago
HEIGHT	5'10"
WEIGHT	12st 4lbs
POSITION	Forward
TRANSFER	22 August 1998 from Aston Villa
FEE	£12.6 million

	Apps	Goals
League '99/2000	32	20

AWARDS Carling Player of the Year 1999

CLUB HONOURS League Cup 1996; FA Cup 1999; Premier League 1999, 2000; European Cup 1999

INTERNATIONAL HONOURS Trinidad & Tobago

THE WINNING SMILE

Yorke's stunning success so soon in his United career quickly put this bad feeling behind him. The fact that he played such a vital part in helping United win the magical treble in only his first season with the club ensured that the famous Yorke grin was wider than ever.

DWIGHT YORKE

One of the hottest footballing topics of recent years has been the explosion in the number of overseas players in the British game. Two concerns are often voiced: first, that the "imported" players are stifling the development of home-grown talent; and second, that some of the overseas stars are past their best and looking for a last big payday on the gravy train of British football.

Zola the maestro

Gianfranco Zola had already turned 30 when Ruud Gullit took him to Chelsea from Parma in November 1996. But it is a tribute to this pocket-sized maestro's marvellous ability that his name is never mentioned when this thorny issue is raised. Quite the reverse, in fact. He is often held up as role model for youngsters - youngsters including the likes of Jon Harley and Jody Morris, England stars in the making.

Instant success

Zola's move to the Premiership reaped instant success, both for himself and for Gullit's side. Chelsea were FA Cup winners in 1997, and Zola was a popular choice in picking up the Footballer of the Year award. He capped a terrific season by scoring the only goal of the game when Italy came to Wembley to play England early in 1997.

Most important goal

His form dipped in his second season at Stamford Bridge. This was put down to injury problems, Gullit's squad rotation system and homesickness - or perhaps a combination of all three. Even so, he still managed to score Chelsea's most important goal for 27 years, the one that brought the European Cup Winners' Cup to Stamford Bridge in 1998.

FA Cup victory

Last season saw something of a goal drought for Zola. He scored just 4 times in the Premiership, and netted only once on Chelsea's glorious FA Cup run - and that was in a 5-0 quarter-final win over Gillingham. Although Gianluca Vialli would no doubt like to see Zola's name on the score-sheet more often, he recognises the value of Zola's creativity and trickery in and around the box. His balance, control, and low centre of gravity help him to twist and turn in the tightest of spots, and he is always aware of his team-mates. He can take credit for countless assists. Zola's season finished on a high when he was acclaimed as one of the key players in Chelsea's FA Cup victory.

Zola may be a supremely gifted footballer, but he is known for the amount of time he spends on the training ground honing his skills. With his talent, dedication and model professionalism, he is someone that any young footballer can watch, admire and learn from.

PLAYER PROFILE

FULL NAME	Gianfranco Zola
DATE OF BIRTH	5 July 1966
BIRTHPLACE	Sardinia, Italy
HEIGHT	5'6"
WEIGHT	10st 10lbs
POSITION	Forward
TRANSFER	15 November 1996, Parma
FEE	£4.5 million

	Appearances	Goals
League '99/2000	32	4
Italy	35	

AWARDS Football Writers Association Footballer of the Year 1997

CLUB HONOURS FA Cup 1997, 2000; League Cup 1998; Cup Winners' Cup 1998; European Super Cup 1998

INTERNATIONAL HONOURS Italy

ZOLA'S EUROPEAN STRIKE Zola had been on the bench for the 1998 Cup Winners' Cup final, against Stuttgart in Stockholm. He came on in the 70th minute and almost immediately raced onto a Dennis Wise through ball. When he planted it high into the net, to the 'keeper's left, he had been on the field barely 30 seconds. The goal gave Chelsea their first European cup success since winning the same trophy in 1971.

GIANFRANCO ZOLA